The Air War in Southeast Asia
Case Studies of Selected Campaigns

by

Herman L. Gilster

Air University Press
Maxwell Air Force Base, Alabama 36112-6428

October 1993

I0155700

Disclaimer

This publication was produced in the Department of Defense school environment in the interest of academic freedom and the advancement of national defense-related concepts. The views expressed in this publication are those of the author and do not reflect the official policy or position of the Department of Defense or the United States government.

This publication has been reviewed by security and policy review authorities and is cleared for public release.

To

Gen Lucius D. Clay, Jr.

Who made this possible

And

My family

Who endured it

THIS PAGE INTENTIONALLY LEFT BLANK

Contents

Photographs

Illustrations

Foreword

Over the years many researchers have analyzed the political aspects of the air war in Southeast Asia. Their studies range from the original *Pentagon Papers* to those published more recently, such as Mark Clodfelter's *The Limits of Air Power: The American Bombing of North Vietnam*. Very little, however, focuses on the economic and operational aspects of the war. The purpose of this book is to fill that void by presenting a set of case studies that subject selected air campaigns during the Southeast Asia era to rigid economic analysis.

In 1970 I presented the opportunity to apply scientific methodology in evaluating the use of air power to Herman Gilster. I asked that he analyze the air campaigns of the Vietnam War, using available data and analytical tools to determine if the Air Force could develop additional insight into air effectiveness for use in future operations.

The basic models Herman developed to describe the campaigns are abstractions or simplifications of the reality that was the air war in Southeast Asia. Therein, probably, lies one of their strongest merits. Numbers do not stand on their own. The quantity of applicable data available from the war in Southeast Asia was nearly infinite, and to be grasped in any meaningful manner there must be a process of abstraction and generalization to delineate clearly basic relationships and interactions. The tools of econometrics and mathematical economics were used because these techniques made the process as efficient as possible. These case studies, which were based on the application of these techniques, take the broadest possible view, thus creating a perspective that should be of interest to high-level decision makers and students of air warfare.

With respect to these analyses, the author advances no claim of infallibility nor did I expect such when I asked that they be accomplished. Practical analysis inevitably must work its way in an expedient manner through the contradictions of the world. At each impasse a judgment must be made; otherwise, the world moves on without the benefit of insights which might have been made available. Hopefully, though, these analyses further illuminate the context within which future judgments take place.

Although I viewed the recent war in the Gulf from afar, it appears that the success of Operation Desert Storm in part was attributable both to the lessons learned during the Linebacker II bombing of North Vietnam (including the call for a single manager for air) and an appreciation of the axiom outlined in "On War, Time, and the Principle of Substitution." Allied forces used air power in conjunction with other forces in fast and dramatic moves that gave no opportunity for the enemy to respond or for the principle of substitution to come into play.

LUCIUS D. CLAY, JR.
General, USAF

About the Author

Dr Herman L. Gilster

Dr Herman L. Gilster (Colonel, USAF Retired) is a 1953 graduate of the US Military Academy at West Point. He received an MBA from the University of Denver in 1957 and an MPA and PhD in economics from Harvard University in 1968. During 26 years in the Air Force, Dr Gilster's duty assignments included five years as a B-47 aircraft commander in the Strategic Air Command; eight years as a tenure associate professor and director of economics instruction at the USAF Academy; four years in operations research at Headquarters Seventh Air Force in Vietnam, Headquarters Pacific Air Forces in Hawaii, and Headquarters USAF in Washington, D.C.; one year as a Federal Executive Fellow in the Defense Analysis Project at the Brookings Institution; and four years as director of international economic affairs in the Office of the Secretary of Defense. After retirement from the Air Force in 1979, Dr Gilster worked with the Boeing Company for seven years, where he served as manager for economic forecasts and analysis.

Dr Gilster has directed numerous economic and systems analysis studies ranging in subject matter from tactical operations to national and international policy. He has been a frequent contributor to the *Air University Review* and other professional journals.

THIS PAGE INTENTIONALLY LEFT BLANK

Chapter 1

Overview

The war in Southeast Asia lasted for nine long years and proved to be the most controversial of all US wars. This book presents five case studies conducted during that war involving three missions of air power—interdiction, close air support, and strategic bombardment.

A major purpose of the book is to pull together these previously classified studies under one cover, set to a central theme based on lessons learned (and relearned) in Southeast Asia. To put the air campaigns in their proper historical context, however, a brief summary of US air participation in Southeast Asia should prove useful.[1]

Air War Summary

Although US air units had participated in the war in Vietnam earlier, major air participation can be dated from congressional passage of the Gulf of Tonkin Resolution in the fall of 1964. Soon thereafter, in early 1965, the US initiated Operation Rolling Thunder and began air strikes against North Vietnam. The campaign began with strikes against lines of communications targets just above the demilitarized zone between North and South Vietnam. Slowly the bombing campaign crept northward toward Hanoi and Haiphong, the major cities of the North, striking not only lines of communications but also petroleum, oil, and lubricants (POL), electrical power, and some industrial targets. These attacks against the North lasted almost four years and were broken by a series of bombing pauses to let the North Vietnamese consider the consequences of further prosecution of the war. Instead, they used the pauses to recover and to strengthen their defenses. The final case study, entitled "On War, Time, and the Principle of Substitution" describes various aspects of this campaign.

On 1 November 1968 President Lyndon B. Johnson, hoping to get peace talks started in Paris, terminated Rolling Thunder. During that three-year and nine-month campaign, US forces had flown some 300,000 strike sorties and dropped more than 643,000 tons of bombs on North Vietnam. With the secession of bombing in the North, attention shifted to the Ho Chi Minh Trail in the panhandle of southern Laos, where the majority of supplies now moved from north to south. Thus began a series of dedicated interdiction campaigns, code-named Commando Hunts, that continued until the North Vietnamese invasion of South Vietnam in the spring of 1972. The first case study provides an overall evaluation of these campaigns, while the second is an in-depth analysis of one particular campaign, Commando Hunt V.

On 30 March 1972 the North Vietnamese invaded South Vietnam, and air resources that had been used on the Ho Chi Minh Trail were shifted to close air support and tactical interdiction roles within South Vietnam. This invasion was the first North Vietnamese offensive in South Vietnam conducted in an exclusively conventional mode—complete with tanks, sophisticated crew-served weapons, and large attack formations. Thus North Vietnamese forces were clearly more vulnerable to air strikes than in the past. The invasion provided the first real opportunity to evaluate US air in the traditional close air support role, the subject of the third case study.

As a result of the North Vietnamese invasion, strikes against the North were again authorized and the Linebacker I campaign began in May. Strikes against interdiction targets and some strategic targets near and around Hanoi and Haiphong had much better results than those in Rolling Thunder, thanks to the development of *smart* bombs. In July peace talks resumed in Paris, and in October the United States again halted bombing of the North because, according to Dr Henry A. Kissinger, "peace is at hand." A two-month deadlock then ensued and led to the initiation of Linebacker II on 18 December. The fourth case study describes the bombing results of this dynamic, concentrated campaign.

On 30 December 1972 the North Vietnamese agreed to resume negotiations, and on 23 January 1973 the Paris negotiators signed a nine-point cease-fire agreement, effective on 28 January. The US war with North Vietnam was over.

Although the campaigns cited above were the main thrusts of air power, the United States also conducted other campaigns within South Vietnam, in Cambodia, and in northern Laos. Throughout the war, US aircraft struck North Vietnamese and Vietcong targets within South Vietnam. In the context of protracted war, the results were impossible to evaluate. Only when the North Vietnamese attacked in mass during the Easter 1972 invasion was a quantitative evaluation possible and even then, as described in the case study, relevant data were difficult to obtain.

In northern Laos, in an operation code-named Barrel Roll, the US supported friendly Laotian forces, mostly Central Intelligence Agency-trained Meo tribesmen, in their quest to turn back North Vietnamese and Laotian communist offensives across the Plain of Jars. Essentially this campaign boiled down to the communists capturing large portions of the plain during the dry season and US-sponsored forces driving them back during the wet season. The US provided forward air controllers and, at times, strike sorties to supplement the Laotian Air Force in support of Gen Vang Pao's tribesmen. Nine years of US air operations in Laos finally came to an end with a cease-fire in April 1973.

Air operations over Cambodia began in March 1969 to destroy North Vietnamese sanctuaries. Then in April 1970 the United States and South Vietnam invaded Cambodia to further decimate North Vietnamese and Vietcong stockpiles. Thereafter bombing attacks continued in support of friendly Cambodian forces and were the last US air strikes of the war in Southeast Asia. On 15 August 1973 an A-7 bomb run marked the end of the longest war in US history.

Case Study Preview

"Air Interdiction in Protracted War—An Economic Evaluation" investigates the results of air interdiction during periods of protracted conflict. Beginning with examples of interdiction results from World War II and the Korean conflict, it updates the interdiction controversy with a focus on the Commando Hunt campaigns waged against the Ho Chi Minh Trail in southern Laos from 1 November 1968 until 30 March 1972. The study includes estimates of enemy supply and daily operational requirements to help evaluate the logistic impact of the Commando Hunt campaigns. These estimates provide little solace to proponents of the long-term supply denial version of air interdiction.

"The Commando Hunt V Interdiction Campaign—A Case Study in Constrained Optimization" provides an in-depth look at one of the Commando Hunts campaigns, Commando Hunt V, which was conducted from 10 October 1970 to 31 May 1971. The author uses the basic tools and principles of economic analysis to evaluate the allocation and effectiveness of air resources employed against the North Vietnamese logistic network in southern Laos. The study provides an interdiction production function (estimated by the technique of regression analysis) which is used in conjunction with Southeast Asia cost factors to derive optimal cost-effective sortie allocations. The study then compares these allocations with those actually flown to determine the relative efficiency with which air resources were employed.

The author conducted the Commando Hunt V study at Headquarters Seventh Air Force in conjunction with three colleagues from the Department of Economics and Management at the United States Air Force Academy—Richard D. Duckworth, Gregory G. Hildebrandt, and Richard M. Oveson. It, along with the first case study, was later published in the *Air University Review.*

"Close Air Support in South Vietnam, 30 March–31 May 1972" evaluates the role of air power during the North Vietnamese Easter 1972 invasion of South Vietnam. During that period US air power responded with strong tactical air attacks in support of largely South Vietnamese ground forces. The study of close air support presents a short scenario of the ground action, followed by a description of the air buildup as US air resources were redeployed back to Southeast Asia.

The author constructed an analytical close air support model for this study and uses it to evaluate both the responsiveness and cumulative impact of air power. The analytical rigidity of this model falls short of that estimated for Commando Hunt V, which was a more structured campaign. The diversity of the 1972 campaign (ground and air action took place throughout South Vietnam) made obtaining data for a more thorough analysis difficult.

The author conducted the study partly in South Vietnam and partly at Headquarters Pacific Air Forces. Gene D. Hartman, a fellow member of the Directorate of Operations Analysis, was a major contributor.

"Linebacker II—USAF Bombing Survey" provides an analysis of Air Force bombing results during the Linebacker II campaign against the North Vietnamese heartland from 18 December to 29 December 1972. Linebacker II represented an air campaign unique to the war in Southeast Asia. Its concentration of power, short duration, and reduced operational restrictions provided the Air Force with an opportunity to demonstrate the totality of its strike capability. Many believe that Linebacker II demonstrated what might have been achieved earlier if the United States had not been hamstrung by self-imposed rules of engagement.

The analysis of Linebacker II presents quantitative comparisons of the strike effort applied and target damage achieved with lessons learned from strikes on each target category. Release system effectiveness and weather tactics are analyzed and actual target damage is compared to prestrike predictions. The report concludes with a discussion of overall lessons learned and a brief assessment of the campaign impact.

The author accomplished the study at Headquarters Pacific Air Forces in conjunction with Directorate of Targets analyst Robert E. M. Frady, who did a superb job evaluating strike results. Maxie J. Peterson of the Directorate of Operations Analysis provided operational support.

The three case studies covering Commando Hunt V, close air support, and Linebacker II focus solely on strike sorties because strike aircraft directly affected enemy target systems and most influenced the objectives selected for each air power mission. One must not forget, however, that behind the strike sorties stood a large support base. This support included, among others, missions involving air refueling, reconnaissance, airlift, and air rescue. During the nine-year war, KC-135 tanker aircraft flew approximately 195,000 sorties, participating in some 814,000 refuelings and off-loading nearly 9 billion pounds of fuel. Tactical reconnaissance aircraft flew some 650,000 missions, tactical airlift transported more than 7 million tons of passengers and cargo within South Vietnam, and air rescue crews saved more than 2,800 downed US crewmen.

The Linebacker II B-52 operations over Hanoi provide an excellent illustration of the important role played by support aircraft. An average wave of 35 B-52 strike aircraft typically was accompanied by nine F-4 and F-105 surface-to-air missile (SAM) suppression aircraft, 20 F-4 MiG cap and escort aircraft, and eight F-4 chaff-dispensing aircraft— approximately a one-to-one strike/support ratio. To provide air refueling for the strike, armada up to 195 KC-135 tanker aircraft were employed.

The final case study, "On War, Time, and the Principle of Substitution," in a sense serves as an epilogue for our experience in the air war of Southeast Asia. It incorporates the findings of the other studies, particularly the important influence of time and substitution in military operations, and puts the Southeast Asia experience in a broader historical context.

This study reviews US experience with strategic bombing during World War II and updates this experience with the results of the bombing campaigns over North Vietnam. Traditionally, nations under attack have effected both product and factor substitution that in large measure attenuated the economic impact of military strikes against their industrial and logistical sectors. Such substitution was used by the North Vietnamese as well as the Germans. Time, however, is a prerequisite for substitution, and this study highlights the critical role played by time in the success or failure of strategic operations during both periods.

The author conducted this study during his appointment as a federal executive fellow at the Brookings Institution in 1974. It was published by the *Air University Review* and favorably reviewed in *The Wilson Quarterly* for its contribution to foreign policy and defense thought.[2]

Notes

1. For a more extensive history of the air war, see Carl Berger, ed., *The United States Air Force in Southeast Asia, 1961–1973: An Illustrated Account* (Washington, D.C.: Office of Air Force History, 1984).

2. "The Case for Blitzkriegs," *The Wilson Quarterly* 4, no. 1 (Winter 1980): 18.

Chapter 2

Air Interdiction in Protracted War—
An Economic Evaluation

United States Air Force doctrine defines three basic combat missions for tactical air power: counter air, close air support, and air interdiction.[1] Counter air operations are conducted to gain and maintain air supremacy by attacking the enemy's combat aircraft, air bases, antiaircraft artillery (AAA), and surface-to-air missile (SAM) sites. Essentially, these attacks are designed to provide all friendly aircraft the capability to operate freely in the airspace above both friendly and enemy territory. The second mission, close air support, encompasses the use of air power in direct support of friendly land forces. Close air support attacks are made against targets of urgent concern in the immediate battle area and require direct and effective integration between the friendly ground and air forces. Finally, air interdiction, the subject of this article, is defined as the systematic attack of an enemy's logistic network for the purpose of destroying, neutralizing, or delaying his military potential (manpower and materiel) before it can be brought to bear effectively against friendly ground forces.

The range of interdiction strikes may span a distance from the immediate battlefield up to, and sometimes including, the enemy's heartland. Normally, these attacks are made at such a distance to the enemy's rear that detailed coordination with friendly ground forces is unnecessary.

Categorization of the functions of tactical air power into the three missions cited already should not conceal the fact that these missions are in no sense mutually exclusive. Nevertheless, mission definition is useful in that it provides a point of departure for any discussion of the impact and effectiveness of major air components. For instance, it is relatively simple to determine the success of the counter air function by

Previously published in *Air University Review* 28, no. 4 (May-June 1977).

noting the ease or difficulty with which friendly aircraft operate overhead. Likewise, the impact of the close air support function can be evaluated with respect to the success or failure of the ground force it supports. Fortunately, these "measures of merit" are tangible, highly visible, and immediately apparent. Consequently, such operations are recognized as viable, productive missions of air power. True, the military services may debate the question of who can most effectively perform these missions, but there is no question of their importance or whether they fit into the spectrum of vital military operations.

The same cannot be said for the third mission, air interdiction. This mission, along with its effectiveness and viability, has been the subject of some of the most intense debates within civilian and military circles in the Department of Defense. Such debates are not surprising because interdiction by its very nature may not carry with it an immediate payoff. In addition, it has been difficult to show, historically, a consistent payoff for the supply denial objective in terms of its impact on the outcome of a campaign. What is observed is merely the ability of the enemy to fight at the current operating level, a level which he may or may not have selected as a result of the burden imposed on him by air interdiction. Without knowledge of the enemy's precise intentions, one finds it virtually impossible to determine whether the interdiction effort seriously limited his capability to operate at a preferred level of activity. Indeed, some insight into the impact of interdiction during World War II has been gained from German records and interviews, but, barring a similar exchange, we will probably never be able to assess with certainty its true impact during the Korean and Southeast Asian conflicts.

World War II to Southeast Asia

Historical reviews of our experience with air interdiction have concluded that the most dramatic successes were recorded when air interdiction missions were complemented by aggressive ground operations on the part of friendly forces. Operation Strangle, the first full-scale, consciously planned interdiction campaign of World War II, is a prime example. Conducted from March through May of 1944 in

Italy, this campaign was initially assigned the optimistic objective of forcing the withdrawal of the German armies from central Italy by denying them essential supplies. This objective was, of course, unrealistic. Only after the Allied ground offensive was launched on 11 May 1944 did the tangible effect of air interdiction become evident. Within three weeks, the four-month stalemate on the ground had been broken, and the German army was in full retreat. The enemy withdrew some 200 miles, suffering an estimated 70,000 casualties, about one-third of his force in Italy.

In an evaluation of this campaign, F. M. Sallagar of the Rand Corporation concluded that success of the Allied forces cannot be attributed to the accomplishment of the supply-denial objective.[2] The enemy transportation network had an estimated capacity of more than 90,000 tons per day while enemy requirements totaled much less than 5,000 tons per day. The stocks of some critical items such as fuel (gasoline and diesel) and ammunition remained fairly level or actually increased during the pure interdiction phase. They declined later when German army consumption rose steeply during the Allied ground offensive but never to the point of creating overall shortages at the front. This is evident in the figures of table 1, extracted from the quartermaster records of the German army for three key dates: (1) 15 March—the start of Operation Strangle, (2) 11 May—the start of the ground offensive, and (3) 30 May—the beginning of the precipitate German retreat.

Sallagar attributes the failure of interdiction to achieve the supply-denial objective to the following factors, most of which were inherent in the tactical situation confronting the Allies and therefore beyond their control.

During Strangle, the major factors were the redundant capacity of the enemy's transport network, especially in the north where the interdiction belt had been placed; German ingenuity in effecting quick repairs, finding alternative routes, and improvising substitutes; the frugal living standards and stringent conservation measures imposed on German armies, coupled with their low consumption rates during the two months while there was no ground action on the front; the intermittent periods of bad weather when Allied air was grounded so that the Germans were able to make repairs and move up supplies; and the lack of an adequate night bomber capability, which made the nighttime relatively safe for repair work and the movement of supplies.[3]

Table 1

German Army Supply Status during Operation Strangle (metric tons)

Item	15 March Stocks	(Average Daily Consumption)	11 May Stocks	(Average Daily Consumption)	30 May Stocks
Fuel	6,500	(380)	6,250	(450)	3,600
Ammunition	32,750	(400)	37,450	(800)	30,550

Source: F. M. Sallagar, *Operation "Strangle" (Italy, Spring 1944): A Case Study of Tactical Air Interdiction,* Rand Report R-851-PR (Santa Monica, Calif.: Rand Corporation, February 1972).

If the above rationale sounds familiar, one should not be surprised. With the possible exception of the last factor, the same list has been fundamental to debates on the viability of interdiction during the Korean and Vietnam conflicts where, as Sallagar states, "we faced an enemy who was definitely not roadbound, whose consumption needs were frugal beyond anything the Germans ever dreamed of, to whom the holding of territory meant little, and who could select the time and occasion when he was willing to fight."[4]

Despite the obvious failure of Operation Strangle to achieve supply denial, Sallagar concluded that the interdiction effort deserved a major share of the credit for the Allied victory. Although interdiction did not achieve its stated objective, it contributed immeasurably to the defeat of the German armies by denying them the tactical mobility that was so essential to them. By the enemy's own testimony, the reduction and occasional paralysis of his freedom of movement contributed more than any other single factor to his defeat. The disruption effected by Allied air attacks overwhelmed the enemy's distribution system, and although the aggregate supply base was sufficient for combat operations, it was impossible for the Germans to position men and materiel at the right place at the right time.

This same pattern—aggressive ground action that forces the enemy to expend men and materiel in battle, overlaid by systematic interdictive air strikes that limit his capability to bring the required replacements into action—has resulted in some of interdiction's most acclaimed successes. The classic example of such a large-scale joint-force operation occurred preparatory to and during Operation Overlord, the Allied invasion of Normandy in 1944. The devastating impact of air strikes during that campaign was best described by Field Marshal Karl von Rundstedt, commander of the German western front:

> After the first few days, I had no hopes of defeating the invasion. The Allied Air Forces paralyzed all movement by day, and made it very difficult even at night. They had smashed the bridges over the Loire as well as over the Seine, shutting off the whole area. These factors greatly delayed the concentration of reserves there—they took three or four times longer to reach the front than we had reckoned.[5]

Despite the theoretical availability of the most elaborate and inter-connected road and railroad network in the world, the German army was unable to match the Allies' cross channel rate of buildup in the battle area. This failure was in large part the result of air interdiction strikes.

Similar successes were recorded during the first year of the Korean conflict, when the United Nations' ground forces were actively engaged with the enemy. Starting in July 1951, however, when armistice negotiations were initiated, a new chapter in the history of air power was opened. As a result of the politically imposed military stalemate that lasted until the cease-fire in July 1953, military commanders were confined in the use of air assets to a new, unfamiliar environment of protracted war. During the ensuing two-year period, a series of special purpose interdiction campaigns was waged on the railroad and highway network to the enemy's rear. Although each of these efforts met with initial success, the general consensus was that these successes were of fleeting nature.[6] The flexibility of the enemy's logistic system, his ability to effect rapid repairs, and his extremely low supply requirements resulting from little or no ground action militated against any lasting success that might have been visualized. Hence, there is no tangible evidence that interdiction significantly impaired the enemy's capability

The armistice negotiations in Korea, from July 1951 until the ceasefire in July 1953, occasioned a new development in the application of air power; use of the air capability was limited to the unfamiliar environment of protracted war. Special purpose interdiction was used on the enemy's railroads and highways but to little permanent effect. Enemy reinforcements were severely damaged at this siding in northwest Korea, April 1952, but the track at right center shows evidence of recent repair, confirming that such reversals were only temporary.

during the two-year stalemate, and without access to his intentions or records, we cannot confirm with certainty the failure or qualified success of the interdiction effort in Korea.

The resulting frustrations, doubts, and differences of opinion over the viability of air interdiction were further exacerbated during the Southeast Asian conflict. Debate raged hot and heavy over the continued support of this expensive but questionable mission. This, of course, was no moot exercise since more than one-half of all combat sorties flown during World War II, Korea, and Southeast Asia were allocated to interdiction operations.

Few experts question the viability of the "tactical" variety of air interdiction which can be closely related to battlefield success. Rather, it is the viability of the "long-term supply denial" version, which characterized US air efforts during lengthy phases of the protracted conflict in Southeast Asia, that has been questioned. Although examples of the former are included, the main thrust of this chapter is directed toward the latter form of interdiction. In particular, it concentrates on an evaluation of the air interdiction campaigns waged for three and a half years in southern Laos. Not only did these campaigns receive the most extensive quantitative documentation of the war but they also provide the purest example of US experience with air interdiction in a protracted conflict.

Air Operations in Southern Laos

Although bombing operations had been initiated earlier, the first full-season interdiction campaign in Southeast Asia was conducted during the summer of 1966 in a belt across the lower panhandle of North Vietnam.[7] In the summer of 1967, the weight of effort shifted north to the enemy's heartland for the purpose of destroying North Vietnamese military and industrial facilities and paralyzing the railroads. The campaign against the heartland was continued until the 1 April 1968 bombing halt again restricted strike operations to the lower panhandle. Then, on 1 November 1968, President Johnson halted all bombing of North Vietnam.

As the result of a contingent agreement with North Vietnam that prohibited movement of men and materiel directly through the demilitarized zone between North and South Vietnam, attention immediately shifted to the Ho Chi Minh Trail in the panhandle of southern Laos, where the majority of enemy supplies moving from north to south now traversed. Thus began a series of dedicated interdiction campaigns, code-named Commando Hunt, that continued until the North Vietnamese invasion of South Vietnam in the spring of 1972. Strikes against the trail had been conducted earlier, but these were generally considered secondary to attacks on primary targets in North

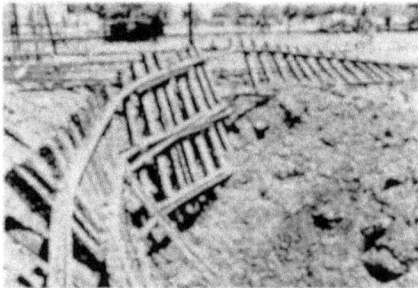

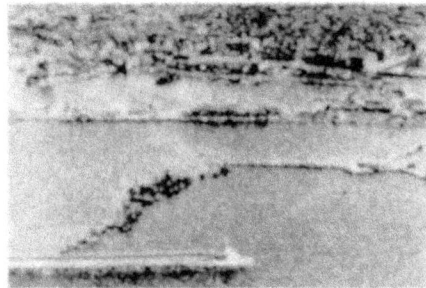

OPERATION STRANGLE

Operation Strangle, whose purpose was "to reduce the enemy's flow of supplies to . . . make it impracticable for him to maintain and operate his forces in Central Italy," was successfully effected in the spring of 1944 through the combined efforts of air interdiction and aggressive ground action. Allied jeeps move through Arezzo following strafing raids by fighter-bombers of the First Tactical Air Force. Power stations were obvious targets as were Mediterranean harbors such as Leghorn choked with wrecked ships after Allied bombings. The destruction of the marshalling yards at Arezzo, a transportation center of central Italy, was yet another challenge to German proprietorship of the peninsula.

Vietnam. The official beginning of the concerted interdiction effort in southern Laos was 1 November 1968.

Geography and Climate

The geographic and climatic features of southern Laos conditioned all aspects of campaign planning, operations, and results. Prominent among the geographic features is the Annam Mountain Range, which forms a natural boundary between Laos and North Vietnam. It is rugged and difficult to traverse, and vehicular entry to Laos is possible only at the major passes. The roads through the passes, however, are normally concealed in clouds; and beyond the passes the tropical forests of Laos provide an almost continuous roof of natural concealment, severely inhibiting both the detection and destruction of targets from the air.

A second critical feature is the climate that is dominated by two major seasonal phenomena—the southwest and northeast monsoons. The southwest monsoon normally predominates from June to October and the northeast from November to May. The climatological patterns for each of the seasons are best remembered with reference to the Annam Mountains. During the southwest monsoon, or wet season, a low-pressure area draws air off the Indian Ocean, bringing thunderstorms and rains to Laos. During the northeast monsoon, or dry season, a high-pressure area blows over the Gulf of Tonkin and South China Sea, bringing low overcast clouds, fog, and drizzle to North Vietnam and dry weather to Laos.

The shifting pattern of the monsoons had an important bearing on the interdiction effort because the enemy geared his logistic flow to it. The northeast monsoons brought improved weather conditions over the roads and made them much more suitable for the movement of men and supplies. Consequently, the enemy concentrated his logistic efforts during these periods, and the interdiction campaigns were planned to respond accordingly.

Ho Chi Minh Trail

These, then, are the characteristic features of the famed Ho Chi Minh Trail, which served as the primary artery for moving North Vietnamese supplies into South Vietnam. The trail's history as a line of communication (LOC) dated back to World War II, when Vietminh bands trekked the same jungle paths. This LOC was developed from the existing footpaths into a highly organized infiltration route for men and supplies. The road network extended from Mu Gia Pass in the north, southward along the heavily forested western slopes of the Annam range, to a series of exit points stretching from just below the demilitarized zone between the two Vietnams, to the triborder region of Laos, Cambodia, and South Vietnam—some 500 kilometers to the south (fig. 1). Although the road net was initially confined to the western slopes of the Annam range, continued expansion of the system pushed additional miles of motorable routes further westward in Laos, providing the enemy an increasingly wide choice of routes along which he could channel supplies. By the summer of 1971, this labyrinth of routes and bypasses encompassed an estimated 3,500 kilometers of motorable roads.

In spite of constant improvement, the roads were still primitive by Western standards, consisting primarily of 18-foot-wide tracks carved out of the jungle. Although both gravel and corduroy surfaces were used to strengthen some sections, the roads were chiefly dirt and nearly impassable during the wet season. The roads were originally built by manual labor, but as time passed, the North Vietnamese made increased use of bulldozers, roadgraders, and other heavy equipment. The route network was operated, maintained, and defended by an estimated 40,000–50,000 personnel organized in geographic area units called Binh Trams. Each Binh Tram had the necessary transportation, engineer, and AAA battalions to ensure movement and security of materiel and personnel in its sector.

The process by which supplies were moved southward was extremely complicated, requiring coordination between various transportation elements and numerous transfers of cargo in and out of vehicles and wayside storage areas. Almost all movement was conducted at night in

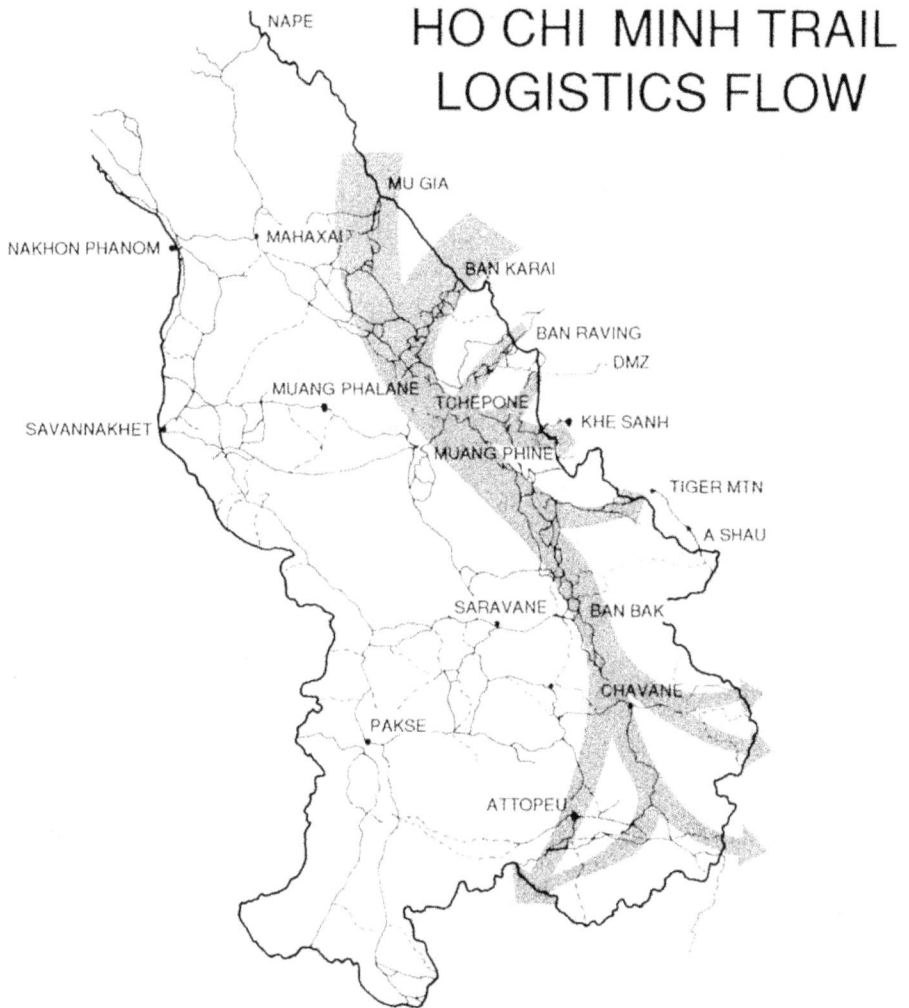

HO CHI MINH TRAIL LOGISTICS FLOW

NAPE

MU GIA

NAKHON PHANOM

MAHAXAI

BAN KARAI

BAN RAVING

DMZ

MUANG PHALANE

TCHEPONE

KHE SANH

SAVANNAKHET

MUANG PHINE

TIGER MTN

A SHAU

SARAVANE

BAN BAK

PAKSE

CHAVANE

ATTOPEU

Figure 1

17

a series of short shuttles, rather than by long-distance hauling. Drivers drove their trucks over the same routes night after night becoming thoroughly familiar with their assigned segments. Periods of high-moon illumination, which allowed travel without headlights, and low cloud cover were exploited to avoid detection from overhead aircraft. Truck movement began shortly after nightfall and normally trailed off about 3:00 a.m. to allow time for the unloading, dispersal, and concealment of supplies and vehicles before daylight. These tactics, developed in Korea and later refined in Laos, might be considered highly inefficient by Western standards, yet they were the most effective way of moving large quantities of supplies in a hostile air environment.

Although the North Vietnamese later made limited use of waterways and pipelines, their road network and trucks remained throughout the war the heart of their logistic system. Intelligence estimates put the North Vietnamese truck inventory in Laos alone at 2,500 to 3,000 during the 1970 and 1971 dry seasons with from 500 to 1,000 moving per night, each carrying about four tons of supplies. Replacement trucks were drawn from large inventories maintained within the sanctuary of North Vietnam in the vicinity of Hanoi and Haiphong. During the height of the interdiction campaigns, the trail logistic system was defended against US aircraft with an estimated 600 to 700 antiaircraft guns.

The Commando Hunt Campaigns

On the US side, a unique feature that distinguished the Commando Hunt campaigns from all previous interdiction campaigns was an electronic detection system that overlaid the enemy logistic network with seismic and acoustic sensors. These sensors were air-delivered devices that detected enemy activity by noting acoustic or seismic disturbances. They were dropped by fighter aircraft in strings of six to eight beside known routes. Each sensor contained a self-destruct feature that was activated by a timer or an antitamper device.

Orbiting aircraft received sensor signals and relayed them to the Infiltration Surveillance Center, where they were analyzed and translated into truck movements. These movements then became the basic index of enemy truck activity. This information was used on a real-time basis to position the interdiction force and on a longer-time basis to analyze trends, compute enemy input and throughput supply tonnages, and assist in the location of truck parks, storage areas, and new roads.

The Commando Hunt interdiction campaigns carried numerical designators that changed with the semiannual monsoon shifts. Odd numbers designated the high-activity/dry season campaigns and even numbers the low-activity/wet season campaigns. Naturally, the dry season campaigns, conducted officially from November to May, received the most attention and study. Enemy logistic activity in southern Laos during the intervening wet seasons was so low that the corresponding military operations could hardly be classified as campaigns.

Summary statistics for the dry season Commando Hunt campaigns are presented in table 2. During the first Commando Hunt, November 1968 through April 1969, the dynamic reaction between opposing forces led to a refinement of the tactics of employing air power in around-the-clock interdiction and prompted development of specialized night attack systems, such as the advanced gunships, which reached maturity in later campaigns and compensated for the gradual withdrawal of other aircraft from Southeast Asia.[8] During the six-month campaign an estimated 45,000 tons of supplies were transported into Laos from North Vietnam, but only about 8,500 tons reached the border of South Vietnam—a throughput/input ratio of 1/5.[9] During Commando Hunt I some 6,000 enemy trucks, the most lucrative interdiction target, were reported to have been destroyed or damaged by US aircrews. These reports do not imply that all 6,000 trucks were permanently disabled, only that they had been hit with ordnance. Statistical estimates indicate that on the average about 60 percent were actually rendered inoperative.

Table 2

Commando Hunt Campaign Statistics

	Commando Hunt I	Commando Hunt III	Commando Hunt V	Commando Hunt VII
Inclusive dates	1 November 1968– 30 April 1969	1 November 1969– 30 April 1970	10 October 1970– 30 April 1971	1 November 1971– 30 March 1972
US Air Strike Sorties (daily average)				
Fighter-Attack	399	288	263	182
Gunship	2	8	11	13
B-52	22	23	30	21
Enemy Resupply Input (tons)	45,000	54,000	61,000	31,000
Throughput (tons)	8,500	19,000	7,000	5,000
Ratio (TP/IP)	1/5	1/3	1/9	1/6
Enemy Trucks Destroyed or Damaged	6,000	10,000	20,000	10,000

Sources: Directorate of Tactical Analysis, Headquarters Seventh Air Force, *Commando Hunt*, May 1969; *Commando Hunt III*, May 1970; *Commando Hunt V*, May 1971, and *Commando Hunt VII*, June 1972.

During the next dry season campaign, Commando Hunt III, the North Vietnamese logistic push during January and February reached new heights and was probably the most intense of the whole war. This effort, which netted a campaign throughput/input ratio of 1/3, may have been inspired by an anticipated loss of the alternate North Vietnamese LOC through Cambodia. Indeed, as the Commando Hunt III campaign was ending, the Cambodians did deny the North Vietnamese use of the port of Kompong Som, through which a large volume of materiel had been flowing. In addition, the allied crossborder penetration into Cambodia during May and June further compounded the North Vietnamese difficulties: large quantities of food and ammunition that had been available to support forces in the southern regions of South Vietnam were lost. Subsequently, the North Vietnamese became actively engaged with Cambodian government forces in operations that further increased their requirement for supplies from North Vietnam.

As a result, the Ho Chi Minh Trail assumed even greater significance as a LOC for enemy men and materiel. With the loss of Kompong Som and the supply line through Cambodia, the trail became not only the supply route for North Vietnamese and Vietcong forces in northern South Vietnam but also the main channel for resupply of enemy forces in southern South Vietnam and Cambodia. Although some leakages through other areas were possible, the Ho Chi Minh Trail remained the last major logistic avenue for the transport of supplies from north to south as the Commando Hunt V campaign approached.

Commando Hunt V was officially inaugurated on 10 October, three weeks early, to seize the initiative prior to the enemy's logistic push into Laos, which, according to intelligence estimates, was to begin on 14 October. The campaign was highlighted by a sustained, concentrated bombing effort in the entry passes to delay and impede traffic flow from October to January, followed by direct air support of the South Vietnamese ground incursion into Laos in February and March, all overlaid with an intensive truck-killing operation throughout southern Laos. More than 20,000 trucks, double the number of Commando Hunt III, were reported destroyed or damaged, and of the estimated 61,000 tons of supplies brought into Laos from North Vietnam, only 7,000 tons reached Cambodia and South Vietnam—a throughput/input ratio of 1/9.[10]

The next dry season campaign, Commando Hunt VII, was inaugurated as usual during the month of November. US forces averaged 182 fighter-attack, 13 gunship, and 21 B-52 sorties per day and reported destroying or damaging some 10,000 trucks through the end of March. The estimated throughput/input ratio was running at a respectable 1/6—5,000 tons output for 31,000 tons input—when the enemy initiated a major invasion of South Vietnam over the Easter weekend. Commando Hunt VII was immediately terminated, and the air resources that had been used on the trail were shifted to close air support and tactical interdiction roles within South Vietnam.

The Estimated Results

The 1972 enemy invasion of South Vietnam brought into question again the overall effectiveness of the interdiction effort in Southeast Asia and leads us back to the beginning. What was the impact of air interdiction on the communist capability to fight in South Vietnam? Unfortunately, no firm quantitative conclusion on the viability of the interdiction campaigns can be advanced. Unlike World War II, there are no supply records or interviews with knowledgeable persons available for assessing true enemy desires and the effect of interdiction on the fulfillment of those desires.

One can only speculate with the use of estimates that may not be completely accurate. Supply tonnages, such as throughput and the enemy's minimum daily logistic requirements in South Vietnam, were routinely estimated, but intelligence analysts admit that these values could be off by a factor of two. Cumulating these values over several years adds another dimension of uncertainty if reporting consistency has not been maintained from campaign to campaign. So although the values presented are best estimates, one should not attribute high accuracy to the absolute stock levels and requirements outlined in the following paragraphs.

Figure 2 gives a profile of estimated amounts of supplies that reached the borders of South Vietnam and Cambodia from the initiation of the Commando Hunt campaigns in November 1968 to the enemy invasion of South Vietnam in March 1972. The seasonal nature of the North Vietnamese logistic effort is readily apparent as is the major supply offensive during Commando Hunt III. It is interesting to note, however, that enemy combat activity in South Vietnam decreased continually throughout this period, including Commando Hunt III, until the major invasion in the spring of 1972. For example, enemy attacks by fire averaged 216 per month during Commando Hunt I, 138 during Commando Hunt III, and 88 during Commando Hunt V. Although some analysts have attempted to relate throughput tonnages with subsequent enemy activity in South Vietnam, there appears to be no correlation between the two. In fact, if one compares data from the Commando Hunt III and VII campaigns, a negative correlation would be implied,

HO CHI MINH TRAIL TROUGHPUT

NOVEMBER 1968 - MARCH 1972

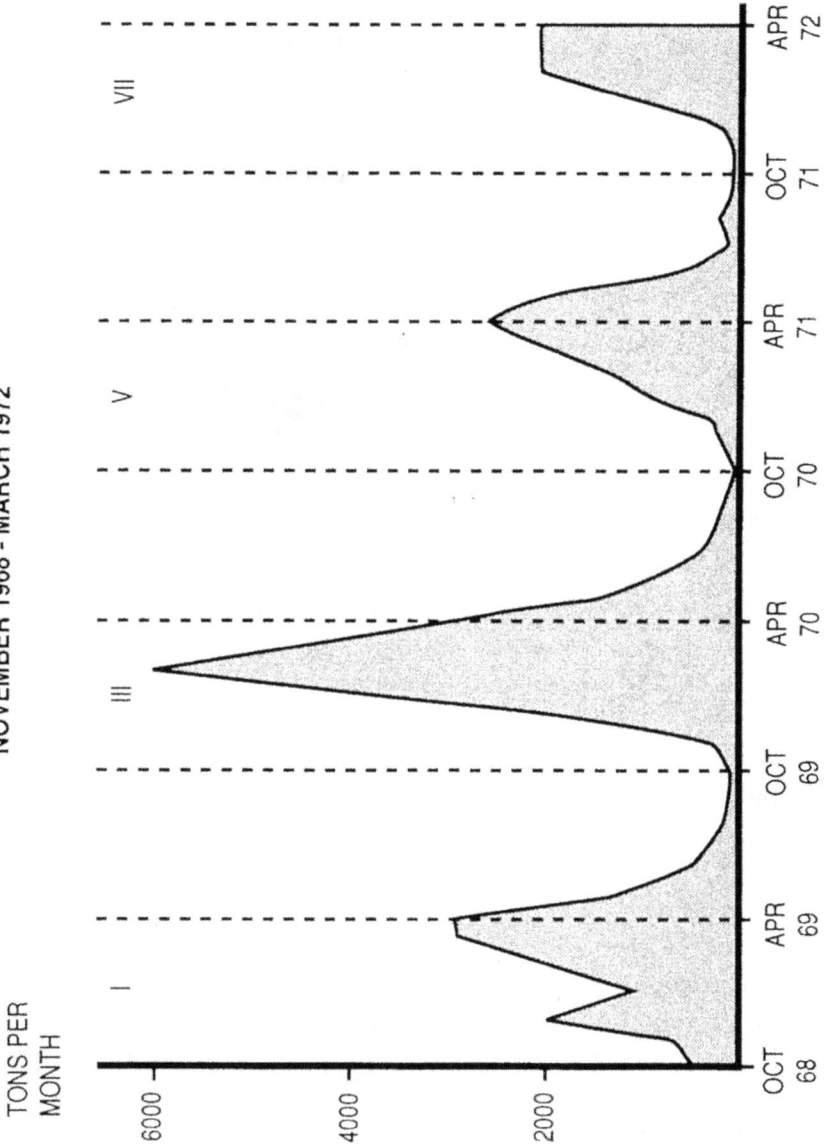

Figure 2

23

Operation Overlord, the code name for the Allied invasion of Normandy on 6 June 1944, was the classic large-scale joint-force operation. Prior to the landing, Allied air forces kept the Luftwaffe in a reduced state, to discourage their sending fighters to France, and in late May and early June made wholesale attacks on French airfields. A-20s pummel a coastal battery captured early in the invasion; Malines rail yard was damaged in an attack on 19 June 1944; a gun emplacement at L'Herbergement was destroyed by Allied bombs.

even though in the northern region of South Vietnam much of the invasion support flowed concurrently through the demilitarized zone and was not the result of a preinvasion effort along the Ho Chi Minh Trail.

Throughput to South Vietnam and Cambodia, of course, is only half the picture. To determine the enemy's supply status, we must also know something of his basic daily logistic requirements to survive and maintain current activity levels. The enemy's minimum requirements were calculated monthly by intelligence analysts of the US Military Assistance Command, Vietnam (MACV), and were predicated on estimated enemy strengths, consumption rates, depreciation, combat activity levels, and the supplies destroyed and captured by ground and air forces during the month. Additionally, these supply requirements were stratified by source based on what portion could be obtained internally in South Vietnam and what portion had to be obtained externally through the borders with North Vietnam, Laos, and Cambodia. Admittedly, these values, based on a number of assumptions, were rough, but they provide some insight into the North

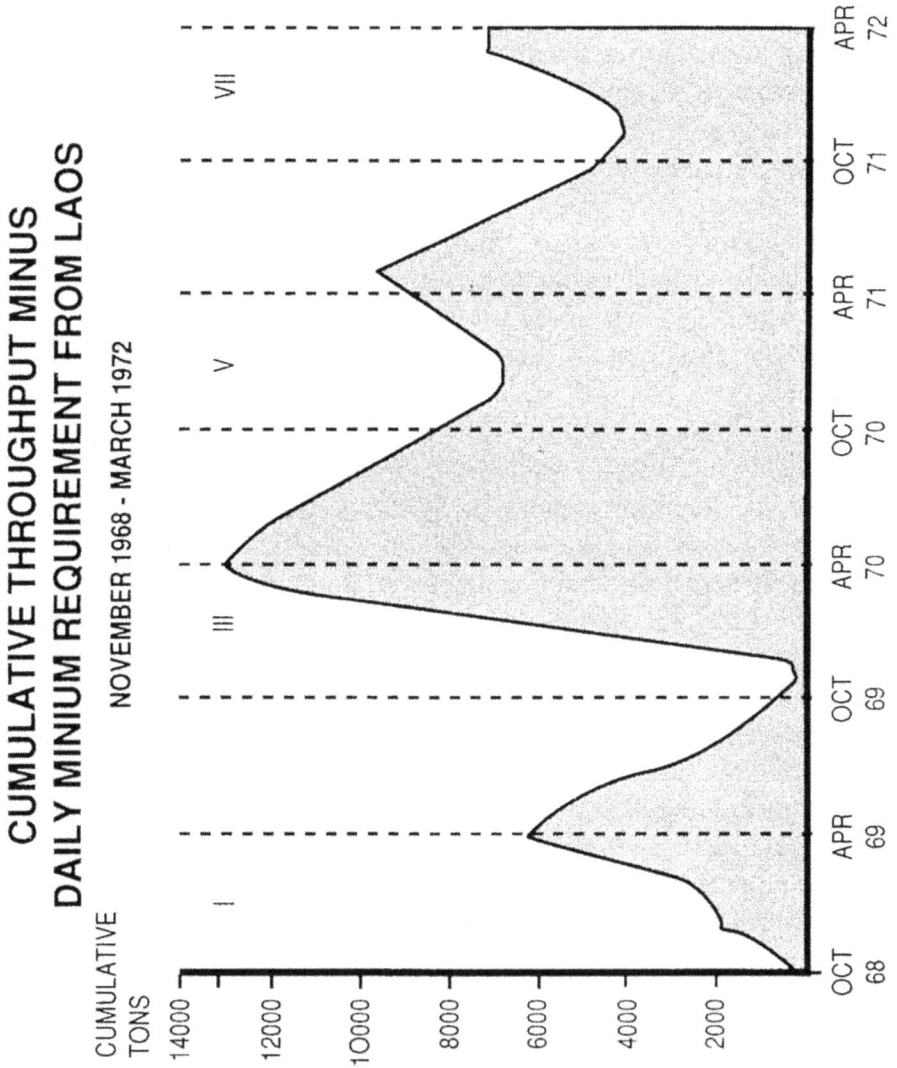

CUMULATIVE THROUGHPUT MINUS
DAILY MINIUM REQUIREMENT FROM LAOS

NOVEMBER 1968 - MARCH 1972

CUMULATIVE
TONS

Figure 3

25

Vietnamese and Vietcong supply requirements—if not in an absolute sense, at least in a relative sense.

Estimated enemy minimum logistic requirements in South Vietnam declined over time from a total of 300 tons per day during Commando Hunt I to about 200 tons per day for Commando Hunt VII. This decrease resulted both from declining enemy strength and activity levels and from revisions in basic consumption factors. The average tonnage requirement was 240 tons per day, of which 205 tons, or 85 percent, was food. The bulk of this food, about 80 percent, was obtained within South Vietnam and Cambodia. The remaining tonnage was comprised of equipment, weapons, and ammunition. Automotive fuel requirements, considered to be minimal, were not included.

The estimated minimum requirements from the trail averaged 35 tons per day, or 15 percent of the total. When combined with throughput tonnages from the trail, these estimates provide the stock profile presented in figure 3. As stated above, caution should be exercised in interpreting the absolute values diagrammed in the figure. The profile depicts the cumulative amount of estimated supplies that flowed through the trail from the beginning of Commando Hunt I minus the estimated enemy minimum requirements from the trail during the same time period. All values are trail-related and exclude internal requirements and acquisitions, flows through Cambodia before the port of Kompong Som was closed in 1970, and the leakages and estimated preinvasion movement of 400 to 800 tons through the demilitarized zone. If throughput were underestimated or minimum requirements overestimated, stock levels from the trail would be higher than depicted; if the opposite were true, the level would be lower. There is, then, a degree of uncertainty associated with the height of the stock profile.

However, if any validity can be attached to the profile, several factors become apparent. First, the North Vietnamese broke about even as a result of the resupply effort during Commando Hunt I and, perhaps as a result of this and the prospective loss of the Cambodian LOC, launched a major supply offensive during Commando Hunt III. After that time, however, the stock level trend became unfavorable to the enemy. We might speculate that the increasingly effective interdiction effort influenced his decision to launch the 1972 invasion of South Vietnam before stock levels again approached zero, but the truth may never be known. The enemy rationale that led to the invasion is but another unknown that contributes to the uncertainty over the impact of the Commando Hunt campaigns.

Second, the profile indicates that the enemy had the logistic capability in March 1972 to launch an offensive in South Vietnam. Certain critics have advanced the argument that the invasion invalidated all previous logistic data because the enemy demonstrated the ability to support an invasion in spite of low throughput predictions. However, the enemy supply requirement from the trail, which contained the weapons and ammunition that could not be obtained elsewhere, was important but not large. It would have been simple to accumulate a sizable supply stock in light of the low-activity levels experienced during previous years. Complete interdiction of a flow of supplies is impossible, and without forced expenditure at the destination, a buildup is inevitable.

This does not mean the enemy was able to position the right supplies at the right place during the ensuing invasion—only that the aggregate tonnage appeared sufficient for an offensive. In fact, estimated throughput from the trail and the demilitarized zone during April and May was 4,600 tons, and the estimated minimum requirement from both was 5,300 tons. This decrease of 700 tons was only 10 percent of the estimated stock level; yet, the enemy offensive had been blunted and was completely contained by the end of May. North Vietnamese objectives, which at a minimum included Hue, Kontum, and An Loc, remained unrealized. From all indications, air power had devastated the enemy's capability to continue the offensive.[11]

This result is somewhat reminiscent of Operation Strangle in Italy, where German aggregate supply tonnages were sufficient for continued operations even after the Allied ground offensive, yet the German defensive posture was broken when tactical interdiction strikes completely overwhelmed the distribution system. It was impossible for German commanders to move and position men and materiel to the right place at the right time. Mobility denial, rather than supply denial, had been the key to Allied success. Supply denial has seldom, if ever, proved to be a viable objective, and the experience in Southeast Asia tends to substantiate the validity of this premise.[12]

Observations

One of the stated objectives of the interdiction campaigns in Southeast Asia was to make the North Vietnamese pay an increasingly greater cost for aggression in the South. Air interdiction, directed at supply denial, does raise the cost of operations to the enemy; but in a limited war context, this cannot be a primary objective. For one thing, the increasing cost argument often leads to a double standard. While US efforts are considered successful if they impose an increasing cost on the enemy, the increased cost imposed on the US by the enemy's initial or counter efforts is not included in the game matrix. (Nevertheless, in the end, US withdrawal from Southeast Asia was predicated, in part at least, on the high cost of continuing the war.) Furthermore, in the North Vietnamese case, the cost to the enemy of replacing bomb damage in southern Laos was largely shifted through external aid to other nations of the Communist bloc. The cost to North Vietnam was mainly the opportunity cost of resources used along the trail. The supplies, trucks, construction equipment, and trained personnel employed in Laos could not be used to rebuild the North Vietnamese economy which had never fully recovered from the 1965-68 bombing campaigns. The fact that North Vietnam continued logistic operations in southern Laos, however, indicates that these costs were bearable.

The increasing cost objective might more appropriately be applied to the December 1972 bombing of the North Vietnamese heartland. This campaign was aimed at applying maximum pressure through destruction of major target complexes in the vicinity of Hanoi and Haiphong. The large, concentrated strike effort severely damaged some of North Vietnam's most important and costly military and industrial facilities.[13] These particular facilities, which are of greatest interest if the increasing cost objective is employed, were previously restricted from air attack. As a result of these restrictions, less valuable interdiction targets along the logistic routes were struck. It is doubtful if the value lost associated with these targets could ever make the cost of continued resupply unbearable.

In summary, increasing the cost to an enemy is a necessary but not a sufficient requirement for an interdiction effort. The constraints associated with limited war, by their very nature, relegate this objective to secondary importance. In the end we must return to the original and basic question: What was the impact of air interdiction on the communist capability to operate at desired combat levels in South Vietnam? From all indications it was negative but within the range of North Vietnamese tolerance. The true impact, of course, is uncertain, but this uncertainty in and by itself militates against the future allocation of air resources to long-term supply interdiction—especially if air resources are limited, as they well may be in light of increasing budget constraints.

Indeed, examples of the vital role played by air interdiction in the success of friendly ground forces have been cited in this text—the campaigns of Europe, the first year of operations in Korea, and the 1972 North Vietnamese invasion of South Vietnam—but in each case the interdiction effort could be directly related to a major ground action. The more intense the action, the more vital became the interdiction effort in forestalling replacements for depleted enemy forces.

However, the timeliness of replacements, a factor so critical to success in intense, large-scale confrontations, fades into relative insignificance as an element in protracted war. Protracted war implies time, and given time, temporary structures rise to replace destroyed bridges, bypasses circumnavigate interdicted route segments, and men and materiel are diverted from less essential to more critical functions. Moreover, in protracted conflicts characterized by guerrilla warfare, only a minimum of supplies is required, and since the option to fight or withdraw remains open, neither the volume nor timing of replacements is paramount to ultimate success.

In concluding, then, it should be noted that air interdiction has been a victim of the type of wars waged in Korea and Southeast Asia, wars that degenerated into protracted periods of relative stagnation. Long-term supply interdiction, the version assigned to cover these static periods, could claim few successes. In fact, it is highly unlikely that any military operation—land, sea, or air—could claim success under such conditions.

Notes

1. Air Force Manual (AFM) 2–1, *Tactical Air Operations—Counter Air, Close Air Support, and Air Interdiction,* 2 May 1969.

2. F. M. Sallagar, *Operation "Strangle" (Italy, Spring 1944): A Case Study of Tactical Air Interdiction,* Rand Report R-851-PR (Santa Monica, Calif.: Rand Corporation, February 1972).

3. Ibid., vii.

4. Ibid., xiii.

5. Basil H. Liddell Hart, *The German Generals Talk* (New York: Morrow, 1948), 243–44.

6. Gregory A. Carter, *Some Historical Notes on Air Interdiction in Korea,* Rand Report P-3452 (Santa Monica, Calif.: Rand Corporation, September 1966).

7. Material on Commando Hunt campaigns was extracted from a series of classified reports prepared annually by the Directorate of Tactical Analysis, Headquarters Seventh Air Force, on the interdiction campaigns in southern Laos. These included *Commando Hunt,* May 1969; *Commando Hunt III,* May 1970; *Commando Hunt V,* May 1971; and *Commando Hunt VII,* June 1972. The extracted material is unclassified.

8. The gunships were C-130 and C-119 transport aircraft modified with sophisticated night detection equipment and 20-, 40-, and later, 105-millimeter cannons to destroy trucks moving down the trails of Laos. These aircraft were by far the most effective truck-killing systems in the US arsenal.

9. Throughput and input were calculated by intelligence analysts who combined the number of southbound sensor-detected truck movements, aircraft visual truck observations, and road and river watch team observations along the Laos entry and exit routes. Duplicate counts were then eliminated to obtain an estimate of the actual truckloads of southbound supplies that entered and exited the system. To the input figure was also added an estimate of equivalent truckloads of supplies that entered Laos through enemy pipelines and natural waterways.

10. See chapter 3.

11. It should be pointed out that the Easter offensive was the first North Vietnamese offensive in South Vietnam that was conducted in an exclusively conventional mode—complete with tanks, sophisticated crew-served weapons, and large attack formations. Thus the North Vietnamese were clearly more vulnerable to air strikes than in the past.

12. One reason that mobility denial tends to be more effective than supply denial is that troop movement requires greater LOC capacity than does supply movement. For example, the road movement of a US infantry division normally consumes six to eight times more road capacity than does its daily resupply requirement. If the movement is by rail, the capacity difference is even greater, averaging about 135 to 1. J. W. Higgins, *Military Movements and Supply Lines as Comparative Interdiction Targets,* Rand Report RM-6308-PR (Santa Monica, Calif.: Rand Corporation, July 1970).

13. For an evaluation of the bombing results, see chapter 5.

Chapter 3

The Commando Hunt V Interdiction Campaign—A Case Study in Constrained Optimization

Military problems are, in one important aspect, economic problems in the efficient allocation and use of resources.

Charles J. Hitch and Roland N. McKean
The Economics of Defense in the Nuclear Age

With these words Hitch and McKean began their classic text, which stimulated decision making based on the principles of economic analysis within the Department of Defense in the early 1960s.[1] Military problems are indeed economic problems in the efficient allocation and use of resources, and this truth became ever more apparent during the long war in Southeast Asia.

Military resource allocation decisions are made in a sequence of steps starting with gross allocations to satisfy national objectives at the highest level and proceeding to specific allocations to satisfy tactical objectives at the lowest. At each step, the decision must be based on the objectives, resources, and limitations specified at the higher level. The lower decisions thus become ones of constrained optimization— maximizing output subject to a given level and use of resources or minimizing the cost of attaining a given level of output.

Such constraint was characteristic of the air interdiction operations in Southeast Asia.[2] With a specified level of air resources, US airmen were asked to reduce the flow of enemy troops and materiel into South Vietnam to the lowest possible level. During most of the war, strikes against the source of supplies in North Vietnam were prohibited, and a

Previously published in *Air University Review* 29, no. 2 (January-February 1978).

relatively inactive enemy in South Vietnam required only a minimal flow of supplies. From the air, US aircrews had to hunt, find, and destroy those supplies along heavily canopied roads through the jungles of Laos. These limitations, among others, make it a difficult, almost impossible mission. To a greater extent than in most previous wars, these men faced a traditional problem in constrained optimization.

This chapter provides an assessment of how well they met the challenge. Basic tools and principles of economic analysis are used to evaluate the allocation and effectiveness of air resources employed during one of the major air campaigns—Commando Hunt V—waged against the North Vietnamese logistic network in southern Laos from 10 October 1970 to 30 June 1971.

The evaluation follows the traditional outline of a microeconomic analysis. First, the product, or interdiction objective, and the inputs that influence that product are defined.[3] Then a discussion of the production function, which relates the inputs to the product, is presented. Following this, the variable cost of applying these inputs based on cost factors derived from our Southeast Asian experience is outlined. And finally, the criterion of attaining the given product at minimum cost is applied to determine optimal air resource allocations. These results are used as a bench mark for measuring the efficiency of the actual Commando Hunt V strike allocations.[4]

The Objective Variable

Correctly specifying the product or objective in an analysis is the most important, yet perhaps the most difficult, task of all. Quantifying that objective only adds to the difficulty. In Southeast Asia, it led to the specifying of a wide spectrum of objectives for air power, at one time or another, often with no clear distinction between input and output. For example, at certain times the total number of sorties flown, a number easily calculated, was taken as the output measure of air power. But sorties are an input, not an output, and maximizing their number can only lead to gross inefficiencies unless constant or increasing returns to scale are experienced.

Another output measure often advocated was target destruction. Although target destruction may be the objective of individual aircraft, it cannot be the final measure of air power. Destruction is a means toward an end, not an end in itself. It is an intermediate product between sorties and the true objective. Therefore, reported target destruction did not play a part in the ensuing evaluation; rather the stated objectives of the Commando Hunt V interdiction campaign were used. The primary objective of that campaign was to "reduce the flow of personnel and materiel into the Republic of Vietnam and Cambodia to the lowest possible level." A secondary objective was to "make the enemy pay an increasingly greater cost for his efforts to dominate Southeast Asia." In a limited sense, the second objective is subsumed by the first. The amount of supplies destroyed along the trail network in southern Laos both added to the enemy's cost and resulted in the delivery of fewer supplies to enemy forces in South Vietnam and Cambodia. *There can be no question, though, that the central purpose of the interdiction force was to reduce the amount of supplies, either by destruction or through forced enemy logistic expenditure, to a level below that at which a sustained enemy offensive in the south could be maintained.* This study, therefore, uses the reduction of enemy supplies that reached the borders of South Vietnam and Cambodia as the basis from which to measure effectiveness of air power in the interdiction role.

The quantitative measure of supplies reaching the borders of South Vietnam and Cambodia was called throughput. Throughput was calculated by intelligence analysts who combined the number of southbound sensor-detected truck movements, aircraft visual truck observations, and road and river watch team observations along the Laos exit routes. Duplicate counts were then eliminated to obtain an estimate of the actual number of truckloads of southbound supplies that exited the system.

To determine whether a reduction of supplies took place in Laos, one must compare throughput with input, or the amount of supplies the enemy put into the system. The estimated number of trucks that entered Laos through the passes from North Vietnam was calculated in the same manner as throughput. To this figure was added an estimate of equivalent truckloads of supplies that also entered Laos through enemy pipelines and natural waterways.

A reasonable measure of the impact of interdiction forces on an enemy logistic system, whether through destruction of supplies or forced expenditure of resources to maintain and defend the system, would be the difference between input and throughput lagged by an appropriate period to account for the length of time supplies are in transit.[5] A lagged structure of the system then becomes important, not because one needs to pinpoint exact transit times, but because it is necessary to determine a reasonable time over which the supplies that entered the system during any time period were subject to air attack.

Logistic intelligence indicated that it normally took the North Vietnamese about six weeks from the start of the dry season in November to fill the Laos supply pipeline and that their shuttle system was probably geared to that time span. A correlation analysis incorporating throughput during a given week and input during previous weeks provided additional support for the six-week estimate as did an area-by-area analysis of sensor-detected truck movements. These same analyses, however, also implied some variation around the predominant six-week transit time. For this reason, a three-week average, rather than a single week's estimate, was used for input and throughput at each end of the six-week period in the construction of the objective variable. This construction is illustrated in figure 4.

Assuming the creation of no permanent stockpiles within the system—and there was no indication of such—one can attribute the primary difference between input and throughput to the interdiction forces. In a reasonable time period, some volume of supplies put into the system did not leave it. In this study, it matters not whether the supplies were destroyed or expended in the maintenance and defense of the system. In either case, those supplies were not available to support enemy offensives in the south.

The Inputs

Next come the inputs to the production function—the resources with which the air commander may influence the objective. Of primary interest in this study are the strike sorties, not only because they

THE OBJECTIVE VARIABLE

$$IP_{t-6} \quad - \quad TP_t$$

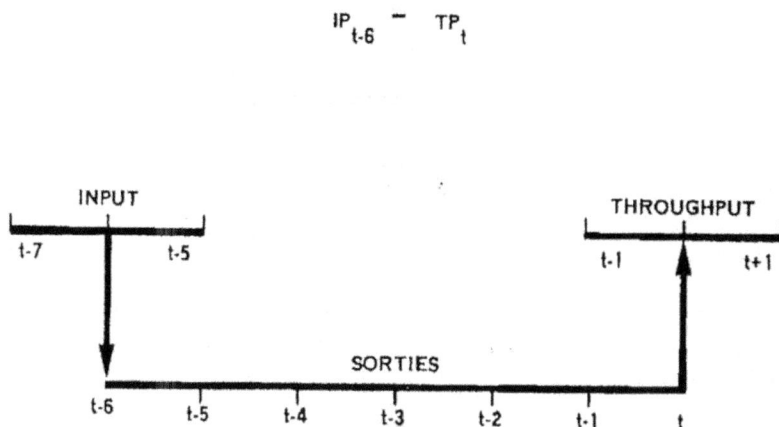

Figure 4

delivered ordnance and directly interfaced with the enemy logistic system but also because they comprised 86 percent of the total variable cost of the interdiction effort. The evaluation, therefore, concentrates on those sorties, which are listed by major aircraft type and target category in table 3.[6] Sorties that did not expend ordnance are not considered strike sorties and are not included.

Throughout the conflict in Southeast Asia, enemy trucks proved to be the most lucrative interdiction target. In fact, there existed a strong statistical relationship between a reduction in throughput (the objective variable) and the number of trucks reported destroyed or damaged, a relationship that could not be found with other target categories.[7] The vital role played by the enemy truck force was recognized in Commando Hunt V, and a concerted effort was made to position the strike force to destroy this critical element. In particular, AC-130 and AC-119K gunships, which were transport aircraft that had been modified with

35

sophisticated night detection equipment and 20- and 40-millimeter cannons, were used to destroy trucks moving down the trails of Laos at night.[8] These aircraft had been developed in previous campaigns and were by far the most effective truck-killing systems in the US arsenal.

Table 3

Commando Hunt V Strike Sorties

Sortie Type	Target Category	Weekly Average
Gunship team (AC-130, AC-119K— with 3 F-4 escorts)	Trucks	65
Fighter-attack (F-4, F-100, A-1, A-4, A-6, A-7, B-57G)	Trucks and storage areas	579
	Lines of communication	695
	Direct air support	404
Bomber (B-52)	Area targets	220

Because of their slower speed and vulnerability, each AC-130 and AC-119 gunship was normally assigned three F-4 escort aircraft to cover its operations over heavily defended areas of the Ho Chi Minh Trail. The primary purpose of these escorts was to suppress enemy antiaircraft artillery activity so that the gunship could continue pursuit and attack of enemy targets.[9] Consequently, the escorts played a major role in gunship results by making possible the operation of this highly effective weapon system in high-threat environments in which it could not normally survive.[10] Since it was statistically impossible to isolate the individual contribution of the escorts from that of the gunship, a gunship team sortie variable was established to act as a proxy for both the gunship and its three escorts. Accordingly, the integrity of the team, or total system concept, was maintained in the subsequent evaluation of weapon system effectiveness.

The fighter-attack aircraft, which with the exception of the A-1 were jet-propelled, were employed against the full spectrum of interdiction targets both day and night.[11] The A-4s, A-6s, A-7s, and some of the F-4s were US Navy aircraft that operated off carriers in the Gulf of Tonkin. The remainder, or about 60 percent, were US Air Force aircraft operating out of land bases in Thailand and South Vietnam. The targets struck by these aircraft fell into three main categories: trucks and storage areas, lines of communication (LOC), and enemy troops and equipment in the vicinity of friendly forces (direct air support).

In the first category, trucks received primary emphasis since storage areas were extremely difficult to locate and attack. Storage areas were kept small, widely dispersed, and heavily concealed; and seldom did an attack provide significant visible results. Sorties against these two targets are treated together because of the command process by which they were allocated. Most sorties were assigned to an airborne battlefield command and control center (an orbiting command post) and forward air controllers over the trail to be directed against either trucks or storage areas, whichever appeared more lucrative at the time. This control feature supports viewing these sorties as an entity.[12] Actually, strikes against both target categories can be classified as attacks of supply destruction as compared to attacks of delay, which are associated with lines of communication sorties.

LOC attacks are attacks against the road network itself. These attacks traditionally ranged from simple road-busting strikes, in which roads were pocked with bomb craters, to much more sophisticated efforts, in which roads were first cratered and then overlaid with magnetic mines to damage road repair equipment and antipersonnel munitions to harass clearance and repair crews. These strikes proved to be the most questionable of all, for unless transport capacity can be rendered and maintained grossly inadequate, attacks of delay may harass an enemy, but they will not seriously restrict his action. The absence of ideal interdiction points in southern Laos and a vast network of interlinking routes and bypasses provided the North Vietnamese numerous options for the movement of supplies. Road busting and mining operations did little to constrain their actions. They quickly bypassed the interdiction points or repaired the roads and continued operations.[13]

LOC sorties, however, were given a new dimension during the initial entry interdiction program of Commando Hunt V. For the first time, both fighter-attack and B-52 aircraft were employed in coordinated, sustained, around-the-clock attacks against the input routes from North Vietnam into Laos. A primary purpose of these attacks was to impede and delay traffic flow until the full complement of AC-130 gunships, which had been in the continental US for modification, could be returned and their new crews acclimated to operations along the trail.

The final strike category, direct air support, was unique to Commando Hunt V. Strikes against enemy troops and equipment in the vicinity of friendly forces are normally viewed as a function of the close air support mission, not air interdiction. During Commando Hunt V, however, the South Vietnamese army staged a major ground incursion against the North Vietnamese logistic network in Laos west of the demilitarized zone between North and South Vietnam. This operation, code-named Lam Son 719, along with several other minor ground operations in Laos, played a vital role in the interdiction campaign, for the purpose of these incursions was not to gain and hold enemy territory but to disrupt the enemy's lines of communication and destroy his supplies. As such, sorties flown in support of these operations contributed to the interdiction objective—the reduction in supplies reaching South Vietnam and Cambodia—and their inclusion as a vital part of the interdiction effort seems appropriate. They are termed direct air support sorties in this study to differentiate them from sorties normally associated with the close air support mission.

The impact of the B-52 aircraft, used in Southeast Asia primarily in a tactical as opposed to the traditional strategic role, could not be evaluated in the analysis because of the aggregate nature of the sortie data and the small variation in the total number of B-52s flown over the trail each week.[14] Evidence of the B-52's contribution to the campaign, however, could be gleaned from other intelligence information, and it might well be that the use of B-52s in conjunction with other tactical air sorties contributed to the positive products noted later.

In summary, the four tactical air sortie sets established as basic input for the production function and subsequent analysis are (1) gunship team sorties; and fighter-attack sorties striking (2) trucks and storage areas, (3) lines of communication, and (4) direct air support targets. To these inputs, it is necessary to add one additional explanatory variable that also influenced the volume of throughput: the enemy intent to push a volume of supplies through during a particular time period. Since actual intent is unknown, one requires a proxy variable to approximate this effect. The variable most highly related to throughput is the number of southbound sensor-detected truck movements, for if the enemy intended to increase throughput during a particular period, this could be accomplished only through an increase in southbound supply movements. Southbound sensor-detected truck movements are, therefore, used to proxy enemy intent and serve further as a normalizing influence so that the effectiveness of the various sortie sets can be more accurately evaluated.

To conform with the lagged structure described in the previous section and the assumption that six weeks was a reasonable period over which air strikes might affect a volume of supplies in transit, moving weekly averages from week t-6 through week t (fig. 4) were calculated for each sortie set. For consistency, a similar moving average was also calculated for the proxy variable, southbound sensor-detected truck movements.

Figure 5 provides a plot of the sortie variables with the horizontal time scale entered at the midpoint of the moving averages. The dynamics of the campaign become quite evident in such a plot. First was the allocation of a major portion of the sorties to the entry interdiction campaign in November and December, then the rather dramatic shift to support the Lam Son 719 ground incursion in February and March. Overlaying these two operations was the increasing level of effort directed against trucks and storage areas as enemy traffic began to surge in December and the gunships returned to the theater.

Figure 6 presents a similar plot for southbound sensor-detected truck movements, derived from the activations of seismic sensors delivered by US aircraft in strings of six to eight beside known enemy routes. This profile provides a good representation of the trend of enemy activity over a dry season campaign in southern Laos. The weekly values, however, include duplicate counts of individual trucks that passed through more than one sensor string in a single night. Therefore, sensor-detected movements should not be viewed in an absolute sense

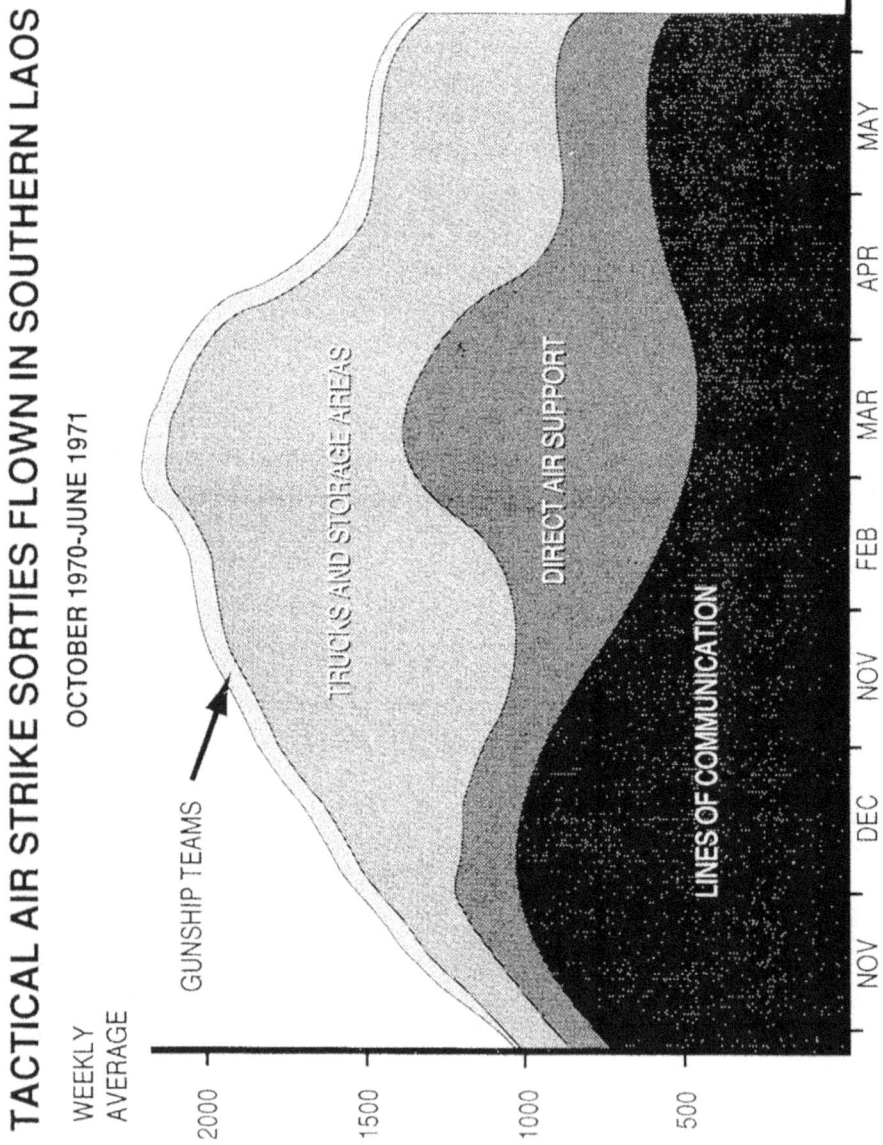

TACTICAL AIR STRIKE SORTIES FLOWN IN SOUTHERN LAOS

OCTOBER 1970-JUNE 1971

WEEKLY
AVERAGE

GUNSHIP TEAMS

TRUCKS AND STORAGE AREAS

DIRECT AIR SUPPORT

LINES OF COMMUNICATION

2000

1500

1000

500

NOV   DEC   NOV   FEB   MAR   APR   MAY

Figure 5

SOUTHBOUND SENSOR-DETECTED TRUCK MOVEMENTS

OCTOBER 1970-JUNE 1971

WEEKLY
AVERAGE

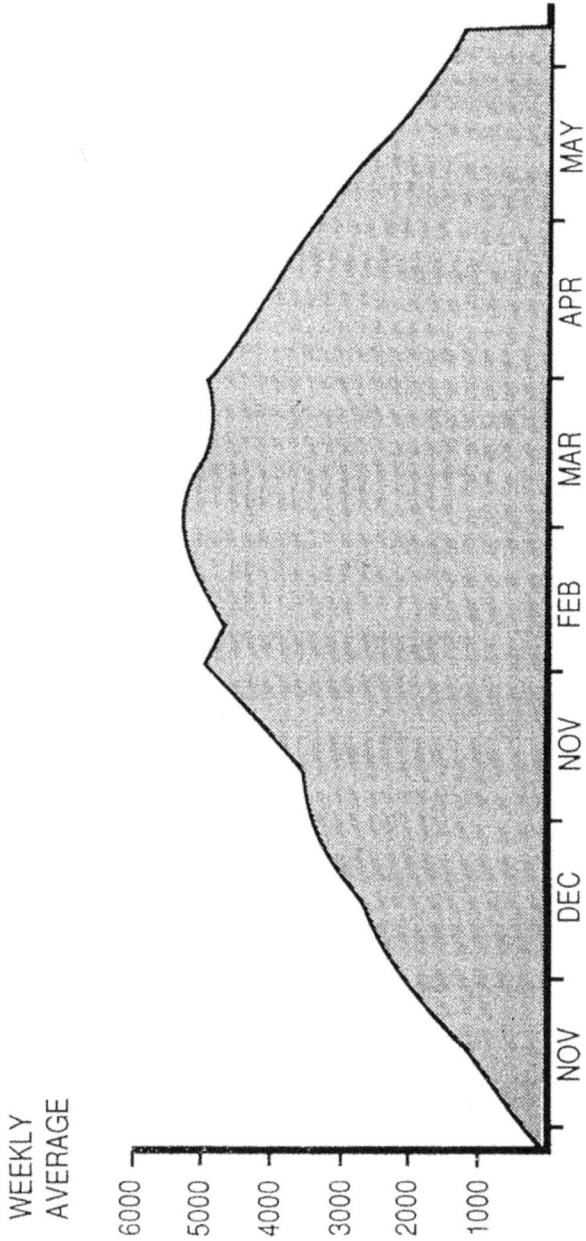

Figure 6

but rather as a relative measure or index of variations in enemy activity over a span of time. As can be seen, during Commando Hunt V enemy activity increased from a wet season low in October, reached a maximum during February and March, and then declined again as the next wet season approached.

The Production Function

At the heart of an economic analysis is the production function, which describes how inputs can be combined to produce the output or objective. In other words, it defines the alternate ways the objective may be attained. The production function that provided the most significant and realistic results was the modified version of the Cobb-Douglas model:

$$Q = X_1^{1.31} \; X_2^{.57} \; X_3^{.33} \; X_4^{.28} \; X_5^{-.85}$$

Where: Q = The objective variable, $IP_{t-6} - TP_t$ per week.

X_1 = Gunship team sorties against trucks per week.

X_2 = Fighter-attack sorties against trucks and storage areas per week.

X_3 = Fighter-attack sorties against lines of communication per week.

X_4 = Fighter-attack sorties in direct air support per week.

X_5 = Southbound sensor-detected movements per week.

The Xs are weekly moving averages week t-6 through week t.[15]

All exponents for the sortie sets are positive and indicate diminishing returns except for the gunship teams. The exponent of 1.31 on the gunship team variable is greater than one and requires some explanation: it indicates that as more gunship sorties were flown, effectiveness increased at a progressive rate (i.e., a 1 percent increase in gunship sorties resulted in a more than 1 percent increase in the objective variable). Two explanations seem plausible. First, when the

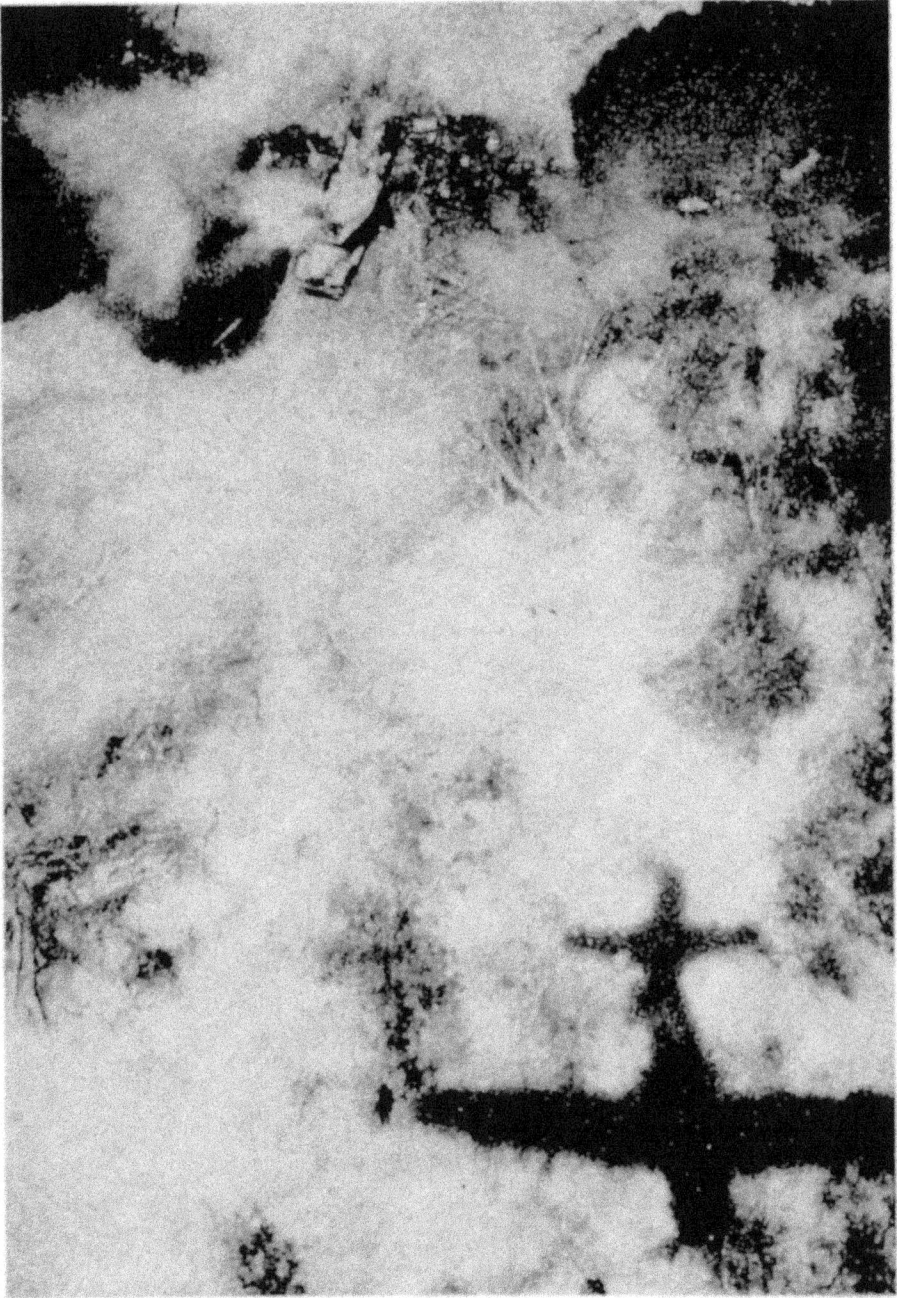

A truck destroyed by an A-1.

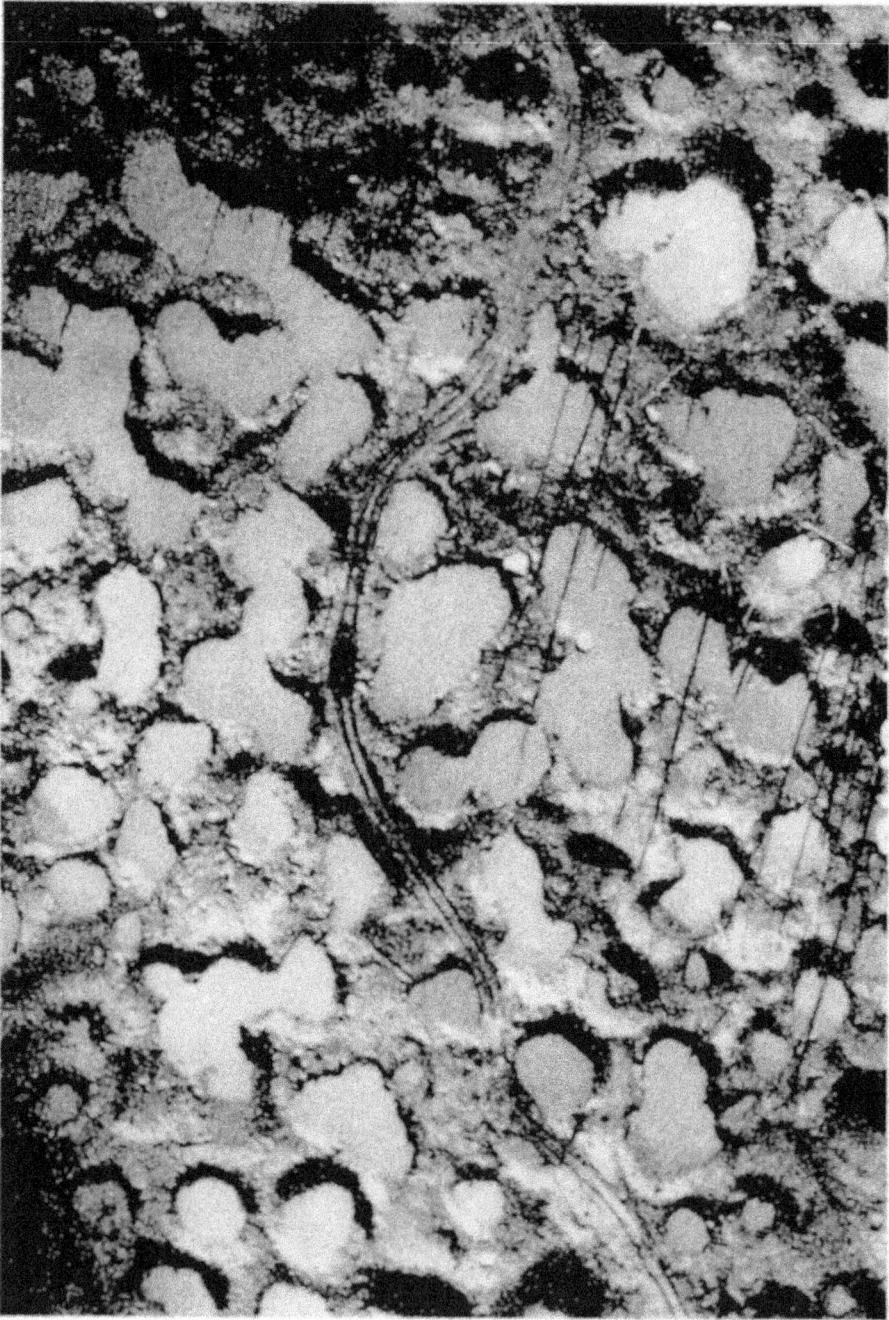

An enemy line of communication winding through bomb craters.

campaign began, few gunships were available and the crews were inexperienced. As the campaign progressed, more gunships were delivered to Southeast Asia at the same time the crews were gaining valuable experience. The exponent may, therefore, incorporate a crew learning curve that was impossible to isolate statistically. Crew learning curves were normally experienced during each dry season campaign since tour lengths were confined to one year.

The second explanation may be that as a gunship force increased, alternate routes the enemy previously used could be covered. This is analogous to the example used to explain increasing returns to the last few radars that close a gap in an early warning line. As long as a gap remains through which the enemy may strike, the radar line is partially ineffective. But as the gap is closed, the whole system becomes effective. Consequently, we receive high returns to the last few radars that secure the system. The extent to which these returns would be experienced further in the gunship case, however, is subject to question. The largest number of weekly gunship sorties flown against trucks during the campaign was approximately 100. To extend the analysis beyond the data base may be inappropriate because beyond some point we could experience diminishing returns as the force is increased, especially if air space limitations become critical.[16]

Of the fighter-attack sorties, the highest exponent is attributed to those that struck trucks and storage areas. This seems reasonable, especially in the case of trucks that had traditionally proved to be the most lucrative Southeast Asian interdiction target. In addition, several rare but spectacular strikes with numerous secondary explosions reported were experienced in storage area attacks during Commando Hunt V. Lines of communication sorties appear to be productive but at a lower level than the first two sets. Previous evaluations of this set of sorties had seriously questioned their effectiveness. It may well be that the complementary use of B-52s for sustained bombing during the initial entry interdiction program resulted in the positive contribution of LOC sorties that was not evident in analyses of previous campaigns. Finally, the productivity of the direct air support sorties probably resulted from their contribution to the joint Lam Son 719 operation, in which the combined air and ground forces destroyed large volumes of supplies and forced the enemy to expend valuable resources in defense. Consequently, these supplies were not available as throughput in subsequent weeks, and the difference between input and throughput, the objective, was increased.

The last variable in the model, southbound sensor-detected truck movements, acts as a proxy for enemy intent. The exponent is negative, which indicates that if sortie levels are not increased when enemy activity increases throughput for any given amount of input will increase. As stated above, the main purpose for including this variable was to isolate and account statistically for the effect of changes in the level of enemy activity, thereby making possible a more accurate comparison of the effectiveness of US air resources.

Variable Input Costs

In examining the conduct of a tactical air operation to determine the most efficient allocation of air resources, one should look only at the variable cost experience and limit analysis to those resources consumed in the actual performance of the mission. Omitted, then, are those costs that cannot be directly related to the operation or to any particular weapon system. These costs are generally defined as fixed costs because they do not vary with the level of combat activity and they are not a direct consequence of flying the mission. Even so, identification of appropriate wartime variable costs is no simple matter. A wide range of alternative assumptions had to be considered, but the choices made in this study suggest that the approximate variable cost of nearly 9 months of interdiction operations in fiscal year 1971 dollars was $1.1 billion, or about $4.2 million a day.[17] These costs are summarized in table 4.

The cost per sortie for fighter-attack aircraft of $8,900 is an average weighted by the number of sorties flown by all fighter-attack aircraft during the campaign.[18] It does not include the F-4 aircraft that escorted gunships since these aircraft were considered an integral part of the gunship team, another weapon system category.

Table 4

Total Variable Cost of the Interdiction Campaign, 10 October 1970–30 June 1971 (FY 1971 dollars)

Aircraft	Total Sorties	Cost Per Sortie ($)	Total Variable Cost ($ millions)
Fighter-attack	62,100	8,900	552.7
Gunship team		52,300	125.5
Gunship	2,400	(11,500)	
F-4 escort	7,200	(13,600)	
B-52	8,100	32,500	263.3
Total strike	79,800	11,800	941.5 (86%)
Total support	49,200	3,100	152.5 (14%)
Campaign total	129,000		1,094.0 (100%)

The gunship sortie cost is also an average weighted by the number of sorties flown by the AC-130 and AC-119K aircraft. The escort sortie cost was higher than the fighter-attack aircraft average since the F-4 was more expensive to operate than the average and the escorts carried large ordnance loads consisting primarily of high-cost flak suppression munitions. In addition, two escorts were shot down during the campaign, giving an attrition cost per sortie twice that of other F-4 strike missions. The variable cost of a gunship team sortie including the three escorts, therefore, was $52,300.

Economic Evaluation

Four of the basic elements of an economic analysis have thus far been examined: The product and inputs have been defined, the production function that relates the inputs to the product has been estimated, and the cost of applying the inputs has been calculated. To complete the analysis and compute an optimal allocation of tactical air resources in terms of Commando Hunt V experience, a criterion must be established to determine which, out of all possible sortie combinations defined by the production function, is the most cost effective.

Since sorties and the objective are not expressed in the same units, the concept of constrained optimization must be employed. It is impossible to both maximize output and minimize cost; maximizing output would call for a prohibitively large force while minimizing cost would call for no force at all. These dual criteria are, therefore, incompatible. As a proper criterion, we may either minimize the cost of attaining a given output or, conversely, maximize output for a given resource or cost level. Because of US interest in the cost aspect of operations in Southeast Asia, the former will form the basis of the economic analysis that follows. An example of maximizing output for a given resource level is also provided.

The optimal allocation of sorties to various target types, therefore, will be predicated on minimizing the cost of the sorties flown per week subject to the constraint that the same average weekly reduction in throughput, $IP_{t-6} - TP_t = 436$ truckloads, reported during the period of October 1970 through June 1971 is maintained.[19] In other words, we require to:

Minimize: The cost of sorties flown per week.

Subject to: $IP_{t-6} - TP_t = 436$ truckloads per week.

Because of the high productivity of the gunship teams, the mathematical solution called for more gunship team sorties than were available to strike trucks at night during the time period under consideration. For this reason, a second constraint was employed to arrive at a realistic solution. Optimum 2 was thus obtained by using the following specification:

Minimize: The cost of sorties flown per week.

Subject to: (1) $IP_{t-6} - TP_t = 436$ truckloads per week.
              (2) Gunship team sorties $= 65$ per week
                  (October 1970–June 1971 average).

The numerical solutions to the cost minimization problems being addressed are given in table 5.[20] Also given, in the column entitled Flown Per Week, are the weekly average number of sorties that expended ordnance during the period October 1970 through June 1971. The total variable cost for this combination of sorties, based on the cost factors cited above, was approximately $18.3 million per week.

Table 5

Cost Minimization Sortie Allocations

Sortie Type	Flown Per Week	Optimum 1	Optimum 2
Gunship team	65	134	65
Fighter-attack			
Trucks and storage areas	579	344	765
Lines of communication	695	201	445
Direct air support	404	167	371
Total	1,678	712	1,581
Cost per week	$18,333,700	$13,345,000	$17,470,000
Saving per week		$4,988,700	$863,300
Marginal cost to reduce throughput		$12,300	$27,300
Marginal value of a gunship team sortie			$187,000

The next column gives the optimal solution in which the number of gunship team sorties was not constrained. This sortie combination would have cost about $13.3 million per week and would have attained, according to the production function, the same reduction in throughput as the combination actually flown. It matters not whether the true reduction was less or more than 436 truckloads; the actual reduction would be identical for the two combinations with the optimum costing some $5 million a week less. The cost of attaining an additional reduction in throughput by one truckload at the optimum with this allocation would be $12,300.

This solution, however, calls for a weekly average of 134 gunship team sorties to be flown at night against trucks in southern Laos. Because of the small number of gunships available at the start of the campaign and commitments to other operating areas and targets in Southern Asia, a weekly average this high was infeasible. It should also be kept in mind that this large number calls for an extension of the gunship team relationship to a point beyond the data base range used in estimating the production model, so the relationship may or may not be valid at this point.

The second solution provides a more realistic optimum by constraining the number of gunship team sorties to 65, the weekly average flown during the period covered by this study. This solution requires 1,581 fighter-attack sorties and is invariant with respect to their cost. In general, about 100 sorties are saved by shifting some sorties from LOC strikes to the more productive strikes against trucks and storage areas. The cost of the Optimum 2 combination of sorties is about $17.5 million, implying a possible saving of somewhat less than $1 million.

The critical role of the gunship team is highlighted in the second solution by the increased marginal cost of obtaining a reduction in throughput by one truckload. As less effective weapon systems are substituted for the gunship team, the marginal cost more than doubles. The dollar value of an additional gunship team sortie in the second solution is $187,000. Thus, total cost could be reduced by $187,000 if an additional gunship team sortie above the 65 were made available. Although this marginal value decreases as more gunship team sorties are added and the first optimum is approached, these results are indicative of the high opportunity cost of using gunship teams in functions other than their primary interdiction role (striking trucks at night).

Such cost does not imply, however, that the gunship team alone should perform the interdiction mission. Critics who advocated the sole use of gunship teams on an average output-per-dollar cost basis neglected a fundamental facet of marginal cost analysis. This facet is illustrated in the Optimum 1 solution of table 5, in which the number of gunship team sorties was not limited. Seven hundred twelve fighter-attack sorties, or 5.4 fighter-attack sorties per each gunship team sortie, were still required for other interdiction functions. Even if the cost of a fighter-attack sortie were 100 percent greater than that used in this study, the optimal distribution would still call for 2.7 fighter-attack sorties for each gunship team sortie. The estimated results, therefore, conform to traditional theory which asserts that the marginal product of one input is predicated in part on the number of other inputs with which it is combined. The gunship team's marginal product was enhanced by the use of other fighter-attack aircraft, as was the marginal product of the fighter-attack aircraft by the gunship teams. Both were an integral part of the interdiction effort.

A second way of looking at an optimal allocation scheme is to determine the maximum reduction in throughput that could be expected from the sorties actually flown. In other words, we now require to:

Maximize: The reduction in throughput ($IP_{t-6} - TP_t$).

Subject to: (1) Gunship team sorties = 65 per week.
(2) Fighter-attack sorties = 1,678 per week.

The solution to this output maximization problem is given in table 6. As can be seen, the potential reduction in throughput is 467 truckloads, 31 truckloads more than was actually attained.

Table 6

Output Maximization Sortie Allocations

Sortie Type	Flown Per Week	Optimum
Gunship team	65	65
Fighter-attack		
Trucks and storage areas	579	810
Lines of communication	695	465
Direct air support	404	403
Total	1,678	1,678
Reduction in throughput	436 truckloads	467 truckloads

The increase in output would result from a 33 percent shift of fighter-attack sorties out of the lines of communication target category to the trucks and storage area category. In the cost minimization problem cited previously, a similar shift would permit a saving of about 100 sorties with the reduction in throughput held constant at the campaign average. In either case, the indication is that fewer lines of communication sorties were required. A reallocation out of this category to trucks and storage areas would have resulted in either an increase in output for the same number of sorties or a saving of sorties for the same output.

In the context of constrained optimization, this imbalance toward LOC sorties is the one fault that can be found with sortie allocations during Commando Hunt V. It was a fault that permeated all of the interdiction campaigns in Southeast Asia—too many attacks of delay in an environment in which time meant little to the enemy. The fact that this sortie set's marginal product was positive, however, indicates a contribution to the interdiction effort that had not been evidenced in other campaigns. If anything, the credit must go to the entry interdiction program, which delayed the enemy's logistic surge and gained time for the buildup and training of the gunship truck-killing force. An earlier termination of this program, however, after first evidence that the enemy's by-pass route structure had been completed, might possibly have resulted in the savings outlined above.

A final aspect of this campaign, one unique to Commando Hunt V, was Lam Son 719 and its contribution to the overall objective. Although the ground incursion did not meet its full expectations, South Vietnamese troops remained in Laos for about six weeks and at one point penetrated as far as Tchepone, a main logistic transshipment hub. The intense enemy reaction to the incursion is indicative of the threat he perceived to his South Vietnamese and Cambodian logistic life lines and his further need to maintain military credibility. Nevertheless, the combined allied air and ground forces destroyed large volumes of supplies and forced the enemy to expend valuable resources in his defense. The productivity of the direct air support sorties resulted from their contribution to this joint operation.

Beyond this immediate effect, Lam Son 719 also played an important role in enhancing the effectiveness of other interdiction sorties. Increased logistic requirements forced the enemy to move and concentrate supplies that might otherwise have been delayed or concealed from air strikes. As a result, the productivity of the entire interdiction force increased, and there was a decided upward shift in enemy truck and supply destruction—indicating once again that when the enemy is forced into a main front confrontation and the timing and volume of replacement men and materiel becomes critical, the effectiveness of an interdiction force is considerably enhanced.

Graphical Review

The problem-solving methodology employed in this case study can be illustrated graphically in a two-dimensional diagram if we group all fighter-attack aircraft sorties into one category and assume they have been efficiently allocated, according to the interdiction model, to trucks and storage areas, lines of communication, and direct air support. We then have only two inputs to consider, the combined fighter-attack sorties and the gunship team sorties, and we seek the least-cost combination of these two inputs to attain the given output—a reduction in throughput of 436 truckloads per week. This is illustrated in the isoquant-isocost diagram of figure 7. The diagram is for illustrative purposes only and should not be taken as an exact reproduction of the cost and output functions. It has also been scaled to better depict the various constrained solutions.

The least-cost combination of sorties is depicted by point A on the diagram where the given 436 isoquant is tangent to the lowest cost line of $13.3 million—the Optimum 1 solution. This solution, however, calls for 134 gunship team sorties, more than were available to strike trucks during the campaign. We must, therefore, move down along the isoquant or equal-output line away from the least-cost solution to point B which is constrained at 65 gunship team sorties—the Optimum 2 solution. As can be seen in the diagram, this solution is achievable only at a higher cost than the first.

If the 1,678 fighter-attack sorties that were actually flown had been optimally allocated between target types, the potential reduction in throughput would have been 467 truckloads. This solution is represented by point C on the higher 467 isoquant and is the example of maximizing output for a given resource level. The 1,678 fighter-attack sorties flown in conjunction with the 65 gunship sorties, however, actually attained a reduction of only 436 truckloads, so their output lies somewhat below the efficient production surface defined by the series of isoquants. The difference, 31 truckloads, is the reduction in throughput foregone, or the opportunity cost of the less than optimal allocation of fighter-attack aircraft.

On a dollar-cost basis, the potential saving available at the Optimum 1 and 2 solutions are the differences between the actual cost line of $18.3 million and the $13.3 million and $17.5 million lines, respectively. If sufficient gunship team sorties had been available, a cost saving of about $5 million per week might have been attained. With the strike resources available, however, a cost saving of less than $1 million per week was possible. This is a rather impressive result. *Compared to the $17.5 million optimal cost, the overrun was only 5 percent.*

Many observers still question the viability and overall impact of the air interdiction effort in Southeast Asia. Historically, it has been difficult to show a consistent payoff for the supply denial objective in terms of its impact on the outcome of a campaign, especially a protracted one. What is observed is merely the ability of the enemy to fight at the current operating level, a level which he may or may not have selected as a result of the burden imposed on him by air interdiction. Without knowledge of the enemy's precise intentions, one finds it virtually impossible to determine whether the interdiction effort seriously limited his capability to operate at the preferred level of activity. Indeed, some

ISOQUANT–ISOCOST PRESENTATION

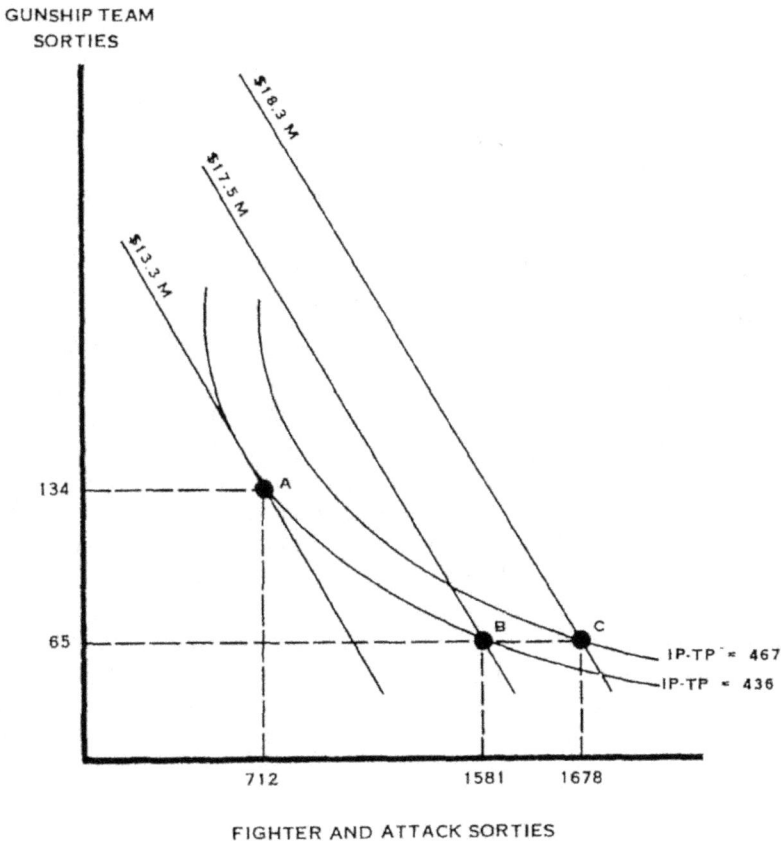

GUNSHIP TEAM
SORTIES

$18.3 M

$17.5 M

$13.3 M

134 ——————— A

65 —————————————————— B   C
                                    IP-TP = 467
                                    IP-TP = 436

712   1581   1678

FIGHTER AND ATTACK SORTIES

Figure 7

insight into the impact of interdiction during World War II has been gained through the media of German records and interviews, but barring a similar exchange, it is unlikely we will ever be able to assess with certainty the true impact during the Southeast Asian conflict.[21]

Nevertheless, this uncertainty should not be allowed to detract from the results already described. US armed forces were deployed by political decree to Southeast Asia, and given this circumstance, a primary task of military leaders was to conduct the assigned operations as efficiently as possible. Within the context of constrained optimization, the phenomenon faced at the tactical level, the final result was as good as could possibly be expected.

Notes

1. Charles J. Hitch and Roland N. McKean, *The Economics of Defense in the Nuclear Age* (Cambridge, Mass.: Harvard University Press, 1960).

2. For background material on the campaigns see chapter 2.

3. The data used in this study are probably as accurate as could be obtained in a wartime environment. The data consisted mainly of sortie counts, which should be highly accurate, and input, throughput, and truck movement estimates calculated by intelligence analysts from electronic sensor activations. Reported target destruction data, often criticized as unreliable, are used only in an auxiliary sense. All data used were first screened for consistency and significant deviations from expected values. In addition, the final economic evaluation was predicated on regression parameters, which are functions of the relationships between variations about data means and not on the absolute values of the means. Therefore, certain absolute data values, such as estimated throughput, might be high or low, but this is of little consequence in a marginal analysis as long as the values were consistently calculated. Since the time span of the study covered only nine months and there were no methodological changes in calculating logistic estimates during that period, a consistency assumption would appear reasonable.

4. These results were originally reported in a classified study, *An Econometric Study of Aerial Interdiction in Southern Laos, 10 October 1970–30 June 1971,* published by Headquarters Seventh Air Force in November 1971. The study was subsequently declassified and reprinted under the same title as USAF Academy Technical Report 77-4, May 1977.

5. Some expenditure of resources, of course, would take place in the absence of interdiction, but most logisticians feel this amount would be negligible in the total.

6. Sortie data were extracted on a weekly basis from the official Southeast Asia Data Base and classified by the first target type struck. During the course of a mission

a few sorties did strike other targets, but in general most expended their ordnance on the same target type. Sorties coded against enemy defenses were primarily gunship escorts and Lam Son 719 flak suppression sorties and were included in the gunship team and direct air support categories, respectively.

7. In a regression equation similar to the type described later, approximately 76 percent of the variation in the objective variable was explained by the number of trucks reported destroyed or damaged.

8. Later, 105-mm cannons were installed on some gunships.

9. Since it was extremely difficult to locate and destroy the well-concealed gun positions, area munitions were delivered in the general vicinity of defense activity to temporarily silence the guns until a strike was completed.

10. On the average, two of the three escorts expended ordnance against enemy defenses in their flak suppression role, and the third principally attacked trucks under direction of the gunship.

11. The B-57G, a small, modified tactical bomber with characteristics similar to those of the fighter-attack aircraft, was also included in this group.

12. The numbers of sorties striking trucks and storage areas were also highly correlated over time. During the beginning and end of the dry season campaign, when the enemy resupply surge occurred, more sorties were normally directed against the enemy's road network or LOCs. During midcampaign, when the enemy resupply surge occurred, more sorties were allocated to strikes against both trucks and storage areas. The resulting high correlation between sorties attacking trucks and storage areas, which for Commando Hunt V was .94, made it difficult to break out their individual influence with any degree of confidence.

13. In the few cases when it was possible to measure road closure time, delays in the range of 0 to 49 hours were recorded with a median of only 15 hours.

14. The weekly mean was 220 sorties with a standard deviation of only 11 sorties. With such a small variation, the marginal contribution of B-52 sorties to the objective could not be estimated.

15. The parameters of the model were estimated using 32 data points or weekly average observations to cover the period of the campaign. The equation accounts for 86 percent (R^2 = .86) of the variation in the objective variable, $IP_{t-6} - TP_t$, and the T ratios for the exponents of the explanatory variables are all significant at the 95 percent confidence level.

16. It should be noted that the production function of this study was estimated using Commando Hunt V data and is unique to that campaign. As with the gunship team case, caution should be exercised in extrapolating any results beyond the range of events that prevailed during Commando Hunt V.

17. Variable input costs included combat aircraft and aircrew attrition, ordnance, and aircraft operating and support costs.

18. These sortie costs ranged from $4,300 for the F-100 to $15,700 for the B-57G. The cost for the F-4, which flew approximately half the fighter-attack sorties, was $10,800.

19. To isolate the sortie contributions, southbound sensor-detected truck movements were also held constant at the campaign weekly average of 3,312.

20. For an explanation of the mathematical technique used to solve problems in constrained optimization, see the *Econometric Study* cited in footnote 4 or any mathematical economics text.

Chapter 4

Close Air Support in South Vietnam, 30 March–31 May 1972

This study describes the effect of close air support on the ground war in South Vietnam during the North Vietnamese invasion from 30 March to 31 May 1972.[1] A large volume of data was examined and much of it was rejected as questionable or not pertinent to the study. To conduct the analysis, it was often necessary to construct additional data using descriptive sources of the ground action.

The analytical models developed are not complete in the sense that they explain the total air-ground picture. This fact, however, does not render the models useless. They were developed to determine if the daily and cumulative number of close air support sorties flown in support of friendly ground forces impacted the enemy's ability to acquire territory in South Vietnam. The analysis leaves little doubt that a significant relationship did exist between the application of air power and reductions in enemy ground gains.

The Ground Scenario

To set the stage for the role of air power, we look first at a brief summary of the ground action. Figure 8 depicts the North Vietnamese Army (NVA) and Army of the Republic of Vietnam (ARVN) main force units at the beginning of the invasion. In military region (MR) I the 304th and 308th NVA divisions crossed the demilitarized zone (DMZ) with the 325th held in reserve. The 324th B Division attacked from Laos toward Hue and the 711th, which was formed in-country, then moved east toward Da Nang. The high point of the NVA invasion in MR I occurred on the first of May with the fall of Quang Tri.

In MR II the 2d and 320th NVA divisions attacked in a pincher movement toward Kontum and the 3d Division moved eastward into

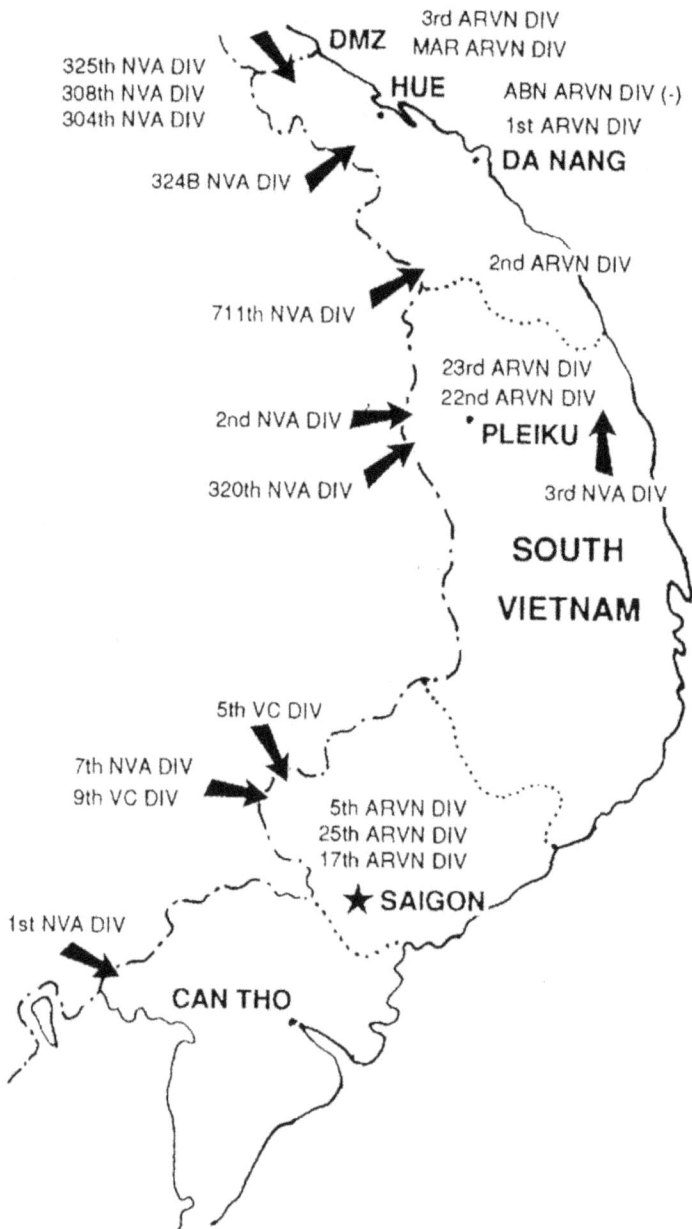

Figure 8. Map of South Vietnam

Binh Dinh Province. The NVA high point in western MR II came on 24 April with the fall of Tan Canh and Dak To. In eastern MR II, the enemy invasion reached its height on 1 May when the NVA essentially gained control of Binh Dinh Province.

In MR III the 7th NVA and 5th and 9th Vietcong (VC) divisions invaded from Cambodia and concentrated on the An Loc area. The NVA high point came on 12 April when An Loc was completely surrounded.

In MR IV enemy activity increased, but since the main body of the 1st NVA Division remained in Cambodia, no main front confrontations occurred. Therefore, this study concentrates on the action and role of air power in the three northern military regions.

US Air Buildup

To counter the invasion, the United States rapidly built up its air power in the area. Table 7 shows US Air Force, Marine, and Navy augmentation of forces already stationed in Southeast Asia. Air Force augmentation during the period came in the timed increments shown. Average augmentation time from Joint Chiefs of Staff (JCS) notification for US-based fighter-attack units was six days. Although specific augmentation times for the Strategic Air Command's B-52 bombers were not made available, the force at Guam was increased by 54 aircraft before the end of April with 13 more arriving the first part of May.

All Marine augmentation came from the Pacific area. The A-4 unit anticipated augmentation and moved from Japan to Subic Point in the Philippines for gunnery practice on 16 May. Notification to deploy to Vietnam came the following day.

The Navy carriers *Constellation* and *Kitty Hawk* were in Japan and the Philippines, respectively, when the NVA invasion occurred. They were back in place within a week bringing Navy strength to four carriers. To maintain four carriers on station, the *Midway* and *Saratoga* were deployed from the US and arrived on the dates shown.

Table 7

US Strike Aircraft Augmentation,
30 March–31 May 1972

Aircraft or Carrier	Location	JCS Notification	In Place	Days Required
USAF				
18 F-4s	Korea	Apr 1	Apr 3	2
36 F-4s	N. Carolina	Apr 6	Apr 11	5
12 F-105s	Kansas	Apr 6	Apr 12	6
36 F-4s	Florida	Apr 26	May 1	5
72 F-4s	New Mexico	May 4	May 12	7
USMC				
26 F-4s	Japan	Apr 6	Apr 7	1
12 F-4s	Hawaii	Apr 10	Apr 13	3
21 A-4s	Philippines	May 17	May 17	-
USN				
Kitty Hawk	Philippines	Mar 31	Apr 3	3
Constellation	Japan	Mar 31	Apr 7	7
Midway	West Coast	Apr 7	May 1	24
Saratoga	East Coast	Apr 8	May 18	40

As a result of the buildup, the number of Air Force, Marine, and Navy fighter-attack sorties flown in Southeast Asia more than doubled from a weekly average of 2,200 during March to nearly 4,700 by the first week of May. B-52 strike sorties increased from about 350 per week to more than 500. Although some strikes continued to be made in Laos, Cambodia, and North Vietnam, the vast majority were directed against enemy ground forces in South Vietnam.

While discussing the US air buildup, we must also acknowledge the role played by the South Vietnamese Air Force (VNAF). Over the years

VNAF had augmented its force to a point where by March 1972 the South Vietnamese were flying 90 percent of the strike sorties in South Vietnam and 43 percent of the effort in Cambodia. After the invasion, VNAF was able to supplement the US air buildup by surging its sortie rate some 30 percent.

Construction of the Model

We now turn to the question of how well air power performed in countering the North Vietnamese invasion. A close air support model was developed and used to evaluate both the responsiveness (the day-to-day effect) and the cumulative impact of air power.

To adequately evaluate the effect of air power, a criterion must be established. A logical measure of the value of close air support is its effect on the ground situation. Therefore, the objective variable selected for this study was the number of strategic ground locations lost to or recaptured from the North Vietnamese Army. These locations included towns, fire-support bases, passes, and other critical points.

A list of strategic points gained or lost by the NVA was compiled from operations and intelligence reports. Because the exact times certain points were evacuated were not known (e.g., whether a loss occurred during the early morning hours or the evening before), a two-day moving average for both enemy gains and air sorties was used to estimate the parameters of the model. As portrayed by the three military region profiles in figure 9, essentially all significant enemy ground gains occurred during April and the first week of May.

Table 8 outlines the variables that were tested and either rejected or used in the model. In addition to the information on enemy ground gains or losses, some measure of how intensely the enemy was fighting was required to evaluate adequately the success or failure of air power on a particular day. One would expect that reported enemy or friendly killed in action (KIA) would provide such a measure. The correlation between KIA and major enemy pushes, however, was insignificant.

MILITARY REGION I

MILITARY REGION II

MILITARY REGION III

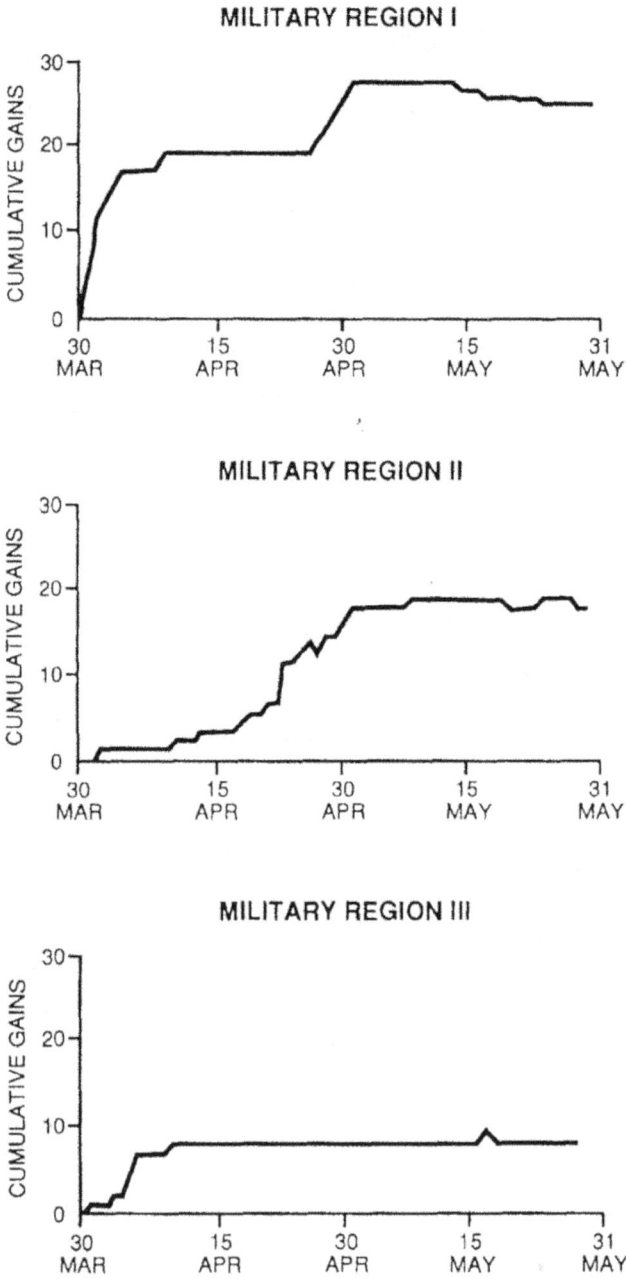

Figure 9. Cumulative Enemy Gains

Some measure of enemy and friendly ground strengths was also desired. Estimated monthly strengths were questionable and were definitely not available on a day-by-day or battle-by-battle basis needed for the model. The best strength variable found was the number of combat maneuver battalions reported daily by the ARVN, but ironically this variable proved to be insignificant or indicated that the more friendly combat battalions in the field, the better the enemy did. Ground contacts and attacks by fire were also checked and rejected because during major enemy pushes few contacts and attacks by fire were reported, whereas during relatively quiet periods when reporting was more complete, a large number might be indicated. The variables that did prove significant are listed in the right column of the table. The construction of these variables is described next.

Table 8

Objective Variable
Enemy Ground Gains or Losses

EXPLANATORY VARIABLES	
Insignificant	*Significant*
Enemy KIA	Enemy Activity Index
Friendly KIA	Weather
Enemy Strengths	Military Regions
Friendly Strengths	Air Sorties
SVA Combat Battalions	—fighter-attack
Ground Contacts	—gunship
Attack by Fire	—B-52

To provide a measure of combat intensity, an enemy activity index which outlined items of significant interest was constructed by reviewing Commander of US Military Assistance Command (COMUSMACV), the Commander of US forces in Vietnam, daily dispatches to US Ambassador Ellsworth Bunker. If enemy activity was cited as high in a particular military region, a value of one was used as

MILITARY REGION I

CUMULATIVE
ENEMY
GAINS

HIGH

MODERATE

| 30 | 15 | 30 | 15 | 31 |
| MAR | APR | APR | MAY | MAY |

MILITARY REGION II

CUMULATIVE
ENEMY
GAINS

HIGH

MODERATE

| 30 | 15 | 30 | 15 | 31 |
| MAR | APR | APR | MAY | MAY |

MILITARY REGION III

HIGH

CUMULATIVE
ENEMY
GAINS

MODERATE

| 30 | 15 | 30 | 15 | 31 |
| MAR | APR | APR | MAY | MAY |

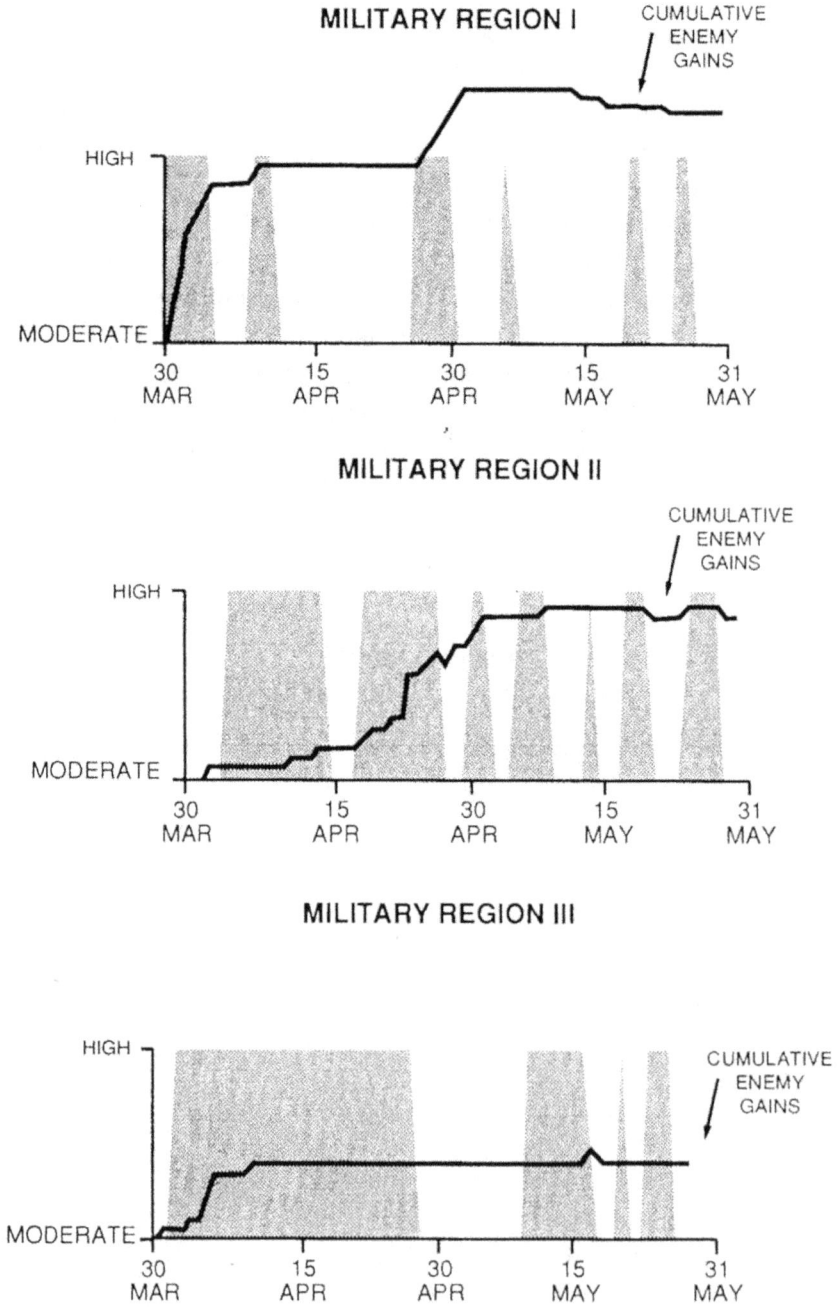

Figure 10. Enemy Activity Index

66

MILITARY REGION I

CUMULATIVE
ENEMY
GAINS

UNFAVORABLE

MARGINAL

FAVORABLE

| 30 | 15 | 30 | 15 | 31 |
| MAR | APR | APR | MAY | MAY |

MILITARY REGION II

CUMULATIVE
ENEMY
GAINS

UNFAVORABLE

MARGINAL

FAVORABLE

| 30 | 15 | 30 | 15 | 31 |
| MAR | APR | APR | MAY | MAY |

MILITARY REGION III

UNFAVORABLE

CUMULATIVE
ENEMY
GAINS

MARGINAL

FAVORABLE

| 30 | 15 | 30 | 15 | 31 |
| MAR | APR | APR | MAY | MAY |

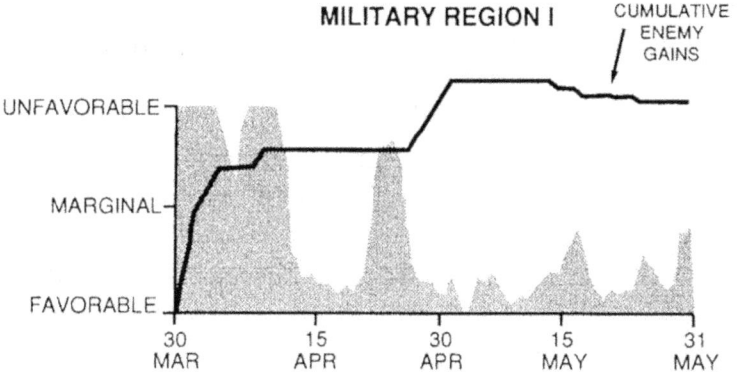

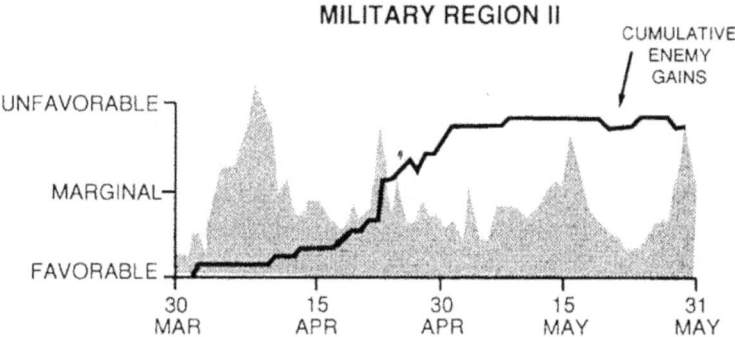

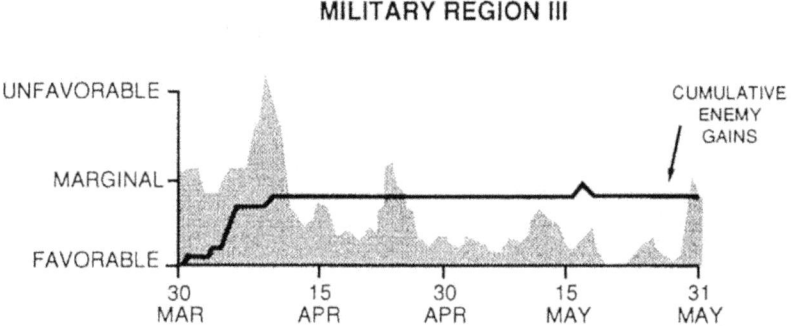

Figure 11. Flying Weather

67

the index level for that day. If activity was cited as moderate or light, a value of zero was assigned. Figure 10 presents the constructed index for each MR (shaded areas) along with the cumulative gain profile for comparison purposes.

Weather also was a significant factor in the enemy's drive to gain territory in South Vietnam. To depict this, a weather index was constructed by categorizing the flying weather for each hour of the day as unfavorable, marginal, or favorable. A value of two was assigned to an hour of unfavorable weather, one to marginal weather, and zero to favorable weather. The hour values were then compiled to provide the weather indices (shaded areas) depicted in figure 11. A comparison with the cumulative gain profile shows that major enemy ground gains generally occurred during days of bad flying weather, particularly in MRs I and III.

As one might expect there was a strong correlation between enemy ground gains, high enemy activity, and bad flying weather. In general the enemy took advantage of bad weather to attack and effect his major gains. In the model described later, the enemy activity index proved to be the stronger variable in describing this effect and was used in lieu of the weather index. It should be remembered, however, that behind the activity index stands the influence of weather.

Geographical locations were also significant in the model, especially MR I which was adjacent to North Vietnam. The final significant variable that affected enemy gains was the number of US and VNAF strike sorties shown in table 9. A daily average of 207 strike sorties were flown in MR I, 137 in MR II, and 185 in MR III. Although MR IV was not included in this study, approximately 61 US and VNAF sorties per day were flown in support of friendly ground force skirmishes in the delta region.

Table 9

**Average Daily Strike Sorties,
30 March–31 May 1972**

	MR I	MR II	MR III	MR IV
Fighter-Attack	179	102	164	59
USAF	82	30	71	14
USN/MC	52	39	52	13
VNAF	45	33	41	32
Gunship	5	7	10	1
USAF	4	3	7	0
VNAF	1	4	3	1
B-52	23	28	11	1
Total	207	137	185	61

Responsiveness of Air

The model was first used to evaluate air power's responsiveness, or impact, on day-to-day ground operations. The estimated close air support model is given below:

		T-ratio
Enemy Gains (Losses)	= .069	
	+ .770 Enemy Activity Index	6.64
	+ .545 Military Region I	4.21
	− .002 Combined Sorties	2.16

$R^2 = .22$

—Enemy gains (losses) and sorties are two-day moving averages.

—Activity index and MR I are qualitative variables.

The parameters of the model were estimated using 186 daily observations (62 days in each MR). The R-squared value indicates that 22 percent of the variation in ground gains was explained by the input variables. Obviously other factors, some not quantifiable, such as ground force morale and leadership, would also explain part of the variation. What was explained, however, is statistically significant at the 95 percent and above confidence levels. The strong positive relationship between enemy gains and the MR I location variable probably reflects the relative ease of reinforcing troops in MR I compared to the other MRs. The negative sign in front of the sortie variable indicates that an inverse relationship did exist between enemy gains and the number of strike sorties flown. As air sorties increased, the number of enemy gains decreased.

The estimated model describes a multidimensional surface that is impossible to visualize, but we can gain an appreciation of the effect of each explanatory variable on enemy gains in a two-dimensional presentation by holding the other sets of variables constant at their mean values. This has been done to depict graphically the effect of air power both when the enemy operated at high and moderate activity levels. As shown in figure 12, the estimated relationship indicates that at a high activity level, and without air, enemy gains would average one per day per MR; but as sorties are increased to near the 250 level, his gains are cut in half. At a moderate level, the break-even point occurs at about 150 sorties.

Cumulative Impact of Air

Next the model was used to evaluate the cumulative impact of air in blunting the NVA invasion. Below is an estimated close air support model similar to the one described previously. This time, however, the cumulative number of sorties was used instead of the daily averages employed in the previous model. It was estimated in the logarithmic form because a curvilinear relationship was implied. As can be seen by the high T-ratio on the cumulative air sortie variable, a strong relationship existed. It is significant at well above the 99 percent confidence level.

DAILY GAINS

DAILY AIR SORTIES PER MILITARY REGION

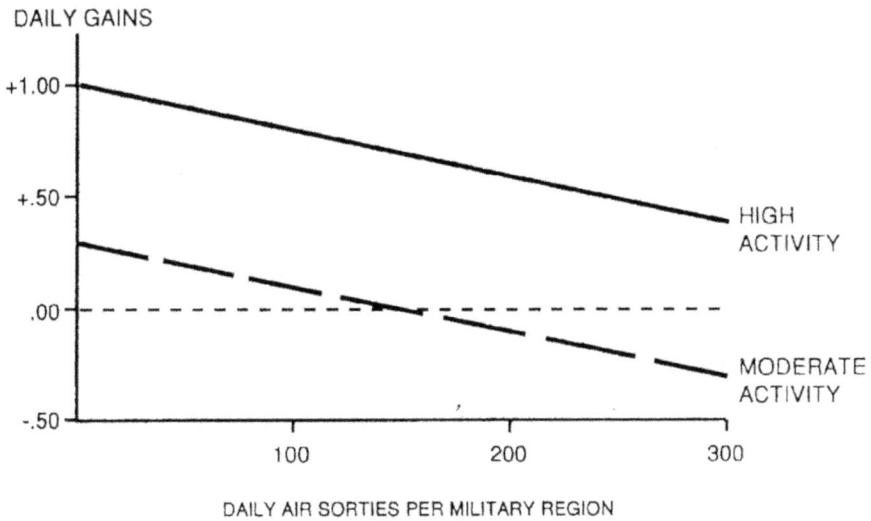

Figure 12. Effect of Air on Enemy Gains

		T-ratio
Ln Enemy Gains (Losses)	= .530	
	+ .529 Enemy Activity Index	5.16
	+ .232 Military Region I	2.12
	− .171 *Ln* Cum. Air Sorties	4.62

$R^2 = .27$

–*Ln* denotes natural logarithmic form of the variable.

By holding enemy activity and the MR I variables constant at their mean values, we see in figure 13 the impact of cumulative air sorties on the number of enemy gains. As the number of strike sorties grew to the 6,000 level in each MR, the number of enemy gains per day approached zero. In general, this level was reached during the first part of May.

The cumulative impact of air power was the devastation of enemy supplies and personnel. In the category of major bomb damage

DAILY GAINS

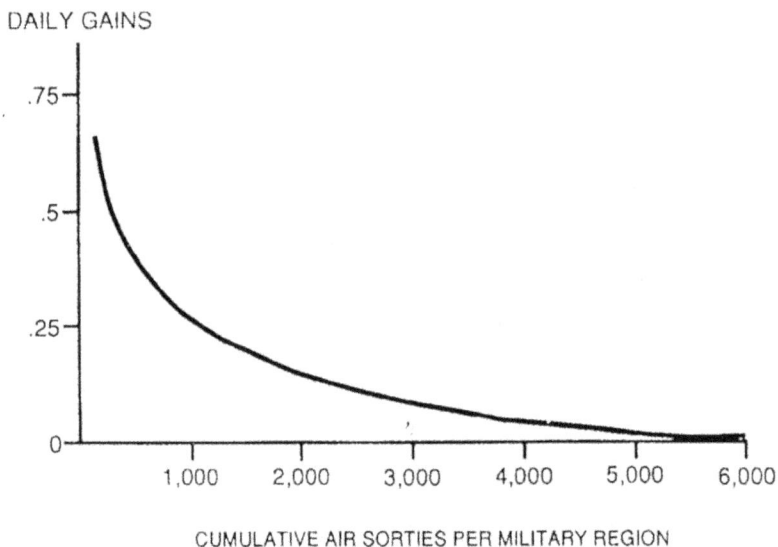

CUMULATIVE AIR SORTIES PER MILITARY REGION

Figure 13. Cumulative Effect of Air Sorties on Enemy Gain

assessment (BDA), 618 gun positions, 521 antiaircraft artillery pieces, 336 tanks, and 1,529 trucks were reported destroyed or damaged by US and VNAF air resources during the two-month period.

Reported enemy KIA figures are suspect, but the total ran to approximately 40,000 during the two months. It is virtually impossible to determine how much of this total could be attributed to air and how much to ground action, since ground follow-ups to air strikes were conducted only infrequently. As an example, through 20 May only 40 follow-ups to B-52 strikes had been made. At that time an average of 25 B-52 cells per day were flying. Unofficial COMUSMACV intelligence estimates, however, did indicate that enemy manpower losses were extremely heavy. Assuming that the main NVA units were 80 percent manned upon entering South Vietnam, and adjusting these strengths for estimated casualties and replacements, main enemy unit strengths approximated the 26 May figures shown in table 10.

Table 10

MACV Estimates of Enemy Strength

Location	Division	26 May Strength
MR I	304 NVA	35%
	308 NVA	36%
	324 NVA	38%
MR II	2 NVA	73%
	3 NVA	53%
	320 NVA	57%
MR III	5 VC	49%
	7 NVA	44%
	9 VC	51%

In summary it appears that North Vietnam suffered a major setback as a result of its imprudent invasion of the South and that air power had a significant impact on the NVA's capability to continue aggression at the level of the first month of the invasion.[2] Sufficient data were not available to drive the quantitative analysis to its logical conclusion and provide a complete air-ground picture. Nevertheless, all evidence indicates that the North Vietnamese failed to meet their objectives, which at a minimum included the imperial capital of Hue in MR I and the provincial capitals of Kontum in MR II and An Loc in MR III. Given these failures in the absence of strong resistance on the part of South Vietnamese ground forces, it seems reasonable to conclude that air power was the determining factor in stopping the enemy's thrust into South Vietnam.

Notes

1. These results were originally reported in a Headquarters Pacific Air Forces briefing dated July 1972.

2. Why North Vietnam chose to make a major invasion of the South in 1972 is still a matter of speculation. Sir Robert Thompson, the British counterinsurgency expert, offers some reasons in *Peace Is Not at Hand* (New York: David McKay Co., 1974), 85–120.

THIS PAGE INTENTIONALLY LEFT BLANK

Chapter 5

Linebacker II
USAF Bombing Survey

Linebacker II was an air campaign unique in the war in Southeast Asia. Its short duration with specific objectives and reduced operational restrictions provided the Air Force with an excellent opportunity to demonstrate the totality of its strike capability. During the 12-day period, 18–29 December 1972, Air Force tactical aircraft and B-52s flew almost half as many sorties in the northern areas of North Vietnam as were flown during the entire previous six months of Linebacker I. The use of B-52s in large numbers was unprecedented, and the large-scale attacks on targets within 10 nautical miles of Hanoi represented a dynamic change in the employment of air resources. Whereas Linebacker I was an interdiction campaign directed primarily at the North Vietnamese supply system, Linebacker II was aimed at sustaining maximum pressure through destruction of major target complexes in the vicinity of Hanoi and Haiphong. The purpose of this study is to determine the degree of success realized by the US Air Force in accomplishing this objective and to delineate methods for improving the probability of success in future air campaigns.[1]

During Linebacker II the Air Force, and particularly the B-52, strike effort was executed in three distinct phases (fig. 14).[2] In the first phase, 18–20 December, the Air Force directed a maximum effort against the Hanoi area using three B-52 waves per night. Continued pressure was maintained throughout the second phase but at a reduced sortie level. Single wave B-52 strikes hit targets along the northeast rail line, most of which were outside the general Hanoi complex. In the last phase, the single wave tactic was continued but at a higher sortie level, and the weight of effort was again directed against Hanoi and Haiphong targets.

Figure 15 depicts the major target complexes struck by both B-52s and tactical aircraft during this period. These complexes included railroad yards, storage facilities, radio communications (radcom)

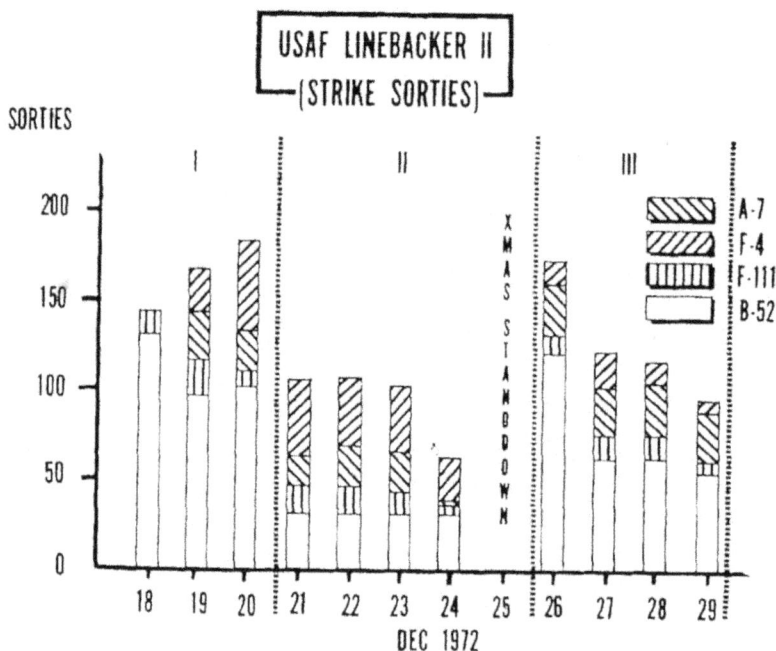

Figure 14

facilities, power facilities, airfields, surface-to-air missile (SAM) sites, and bridges. In all, 59 designated targets were struck by 1,364 Air Force strike sorties during Linebacker II with the sortie weight of effort ranging from a high of 36 percent against railroad yards to somewhat less than 1 percent against bridges (fig. 16). The following section discusses the results achieved and lessons learned from strikes against each target category.[3]

Bombing Results by Target Category

Pacific Air Forces (PACAF) photo interpreters estimated the percentage of damage sustained by each target during Linebacker II from pre- and poststrike photography.[4] The photo interpreters strived to be as consistent as possible in their assessments. These assessments are used throughout this study and, needless to say, the validity of the quantitative evaluations is predicated on the success realized by the photo interpreters in assessing target damage uniformly. The major findings, however, appear to be insensitive to a wide range of subjectivity.

Railroad Yards

The target category that received the largest Air Force strike effort was railroad yards and complexes. The 13 targets struck in this category accounted for 36 percent of the total US Air Force sortie effort. Four hundred eighty-four sorties against these targets delivered over 18,000 bombs.

The results achieved and effort expended against each individual target in this study is illustrated on a set of figures similar to figures 17 and 18. US Air Force level of effort is normally measured by the number of sorties directed against enemy targets, and this convention is continued in this report. In this case, however, with both B-52s and

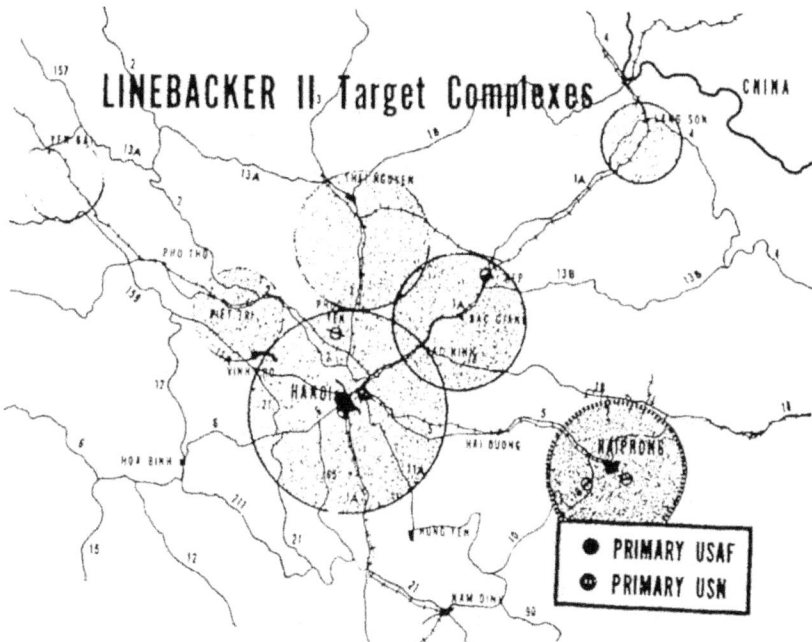

Figure 15

USAF LINEBACKER II STRIKE SORTIES
BY TARGET TYPE
18-29 DECEMBER 1972

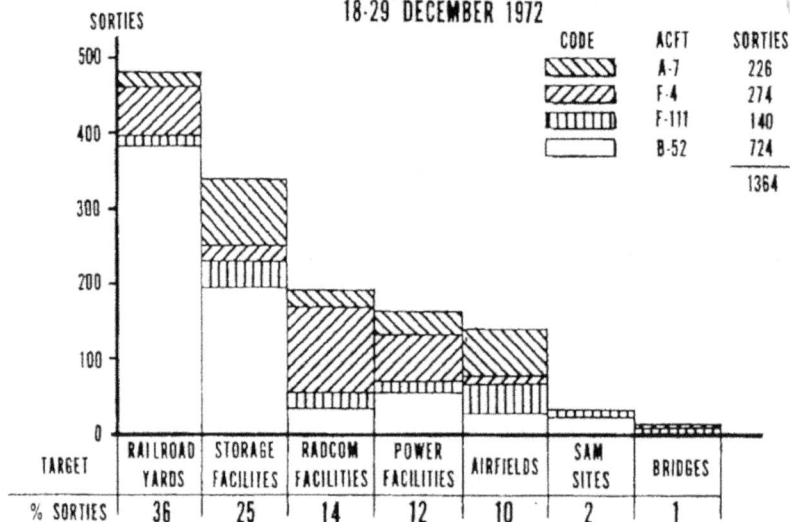

SORTIES

	CODE	ACFT	SORTIES
	∖∖∖∖∖	A-7	226
	⧄⧄⧄	F-4	274
	⟦⟧⟦⟧	F-111	140
	▭	B-52	724
			1364

TARGET	RAILROAD YARDS	STORAGE FACILITES	RADCOM FACILITIES	POWER FACILITIES	AIRFIELDS	SAM SITES	BRIDGES
% SORTIES	36	25	14	12	10	2	1

Figure 16

fighter-attack aircraft contributing, greater insight can be gained when damage is compared to numbers of bombs and the release system used. Therefore, both presentations are given for each target category.

B-52s and F-111s, both all-weather systems, bombed at night using their radar. All-weather long-range aid to navigation (LORAN) bombing for fighter-attack aircraft was based on position fixes over the target determined through long-range navigational equipment. An F-4 Pathfinder with LORAN capability led non-LORAN aircraft to the target and all released bombs on its signal. In good weather, F-4s and A-7s bombed visually, with those F-4s possessing laser capability using laser guided bombs (LGB).

For each target, the left black bar depicts the percentage damage to that target as determined by intelligence photo interpreters. These bars correspond to the left vertical scale. The right bars depict the weight of effort expended against the target and correspond to the scale on the right vertical axis. On the top figure, the right bar indicates the number of sorties applied against the target by aircraft type; whereas, on the bottom figure, the right bar depicts the number of bombs delivered against the target by release system.

Similar figures are presented for each target category. One should note that the damage scale on the left axis remains unchanged from one category to the next, but the right scale varies, depending on the level of effort applied against a particular target category. Therefore, caution should be exercised in making direct comparisons between target categories without reference to the right-hand scale.

The highest overall damage achieved against any target category during Linebacker II proved to be against railroad yards. A damage level of 60 percent or better was achieved against two-thirds of these targets which were the most important rail facilities, other than bridges, in North Vietnam. In addition to the significant facility and rail damage, the strikes destroyed or damaged a large quantity of rolling stock which seriously hampered movement of supplies by rail. Moreover, covered

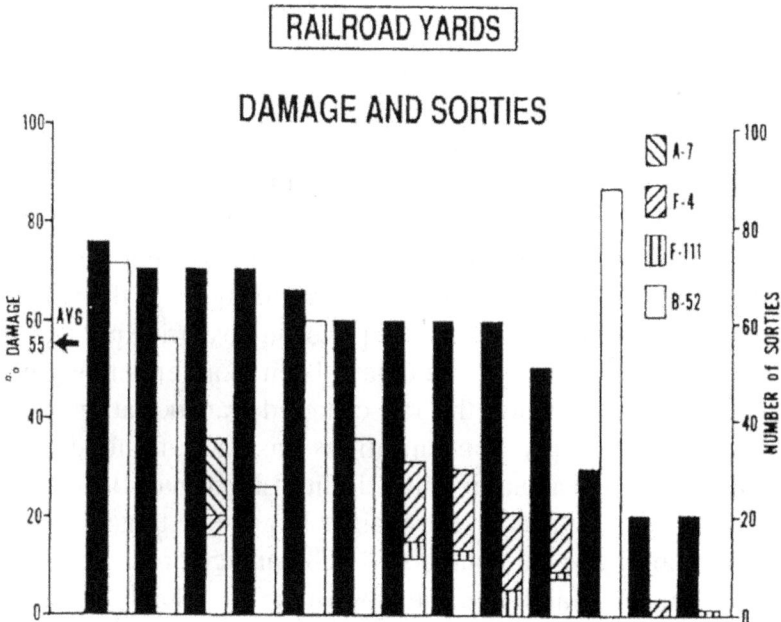

Figure 17

RAILROAD YARDS

DAMAGE AND BOMBS

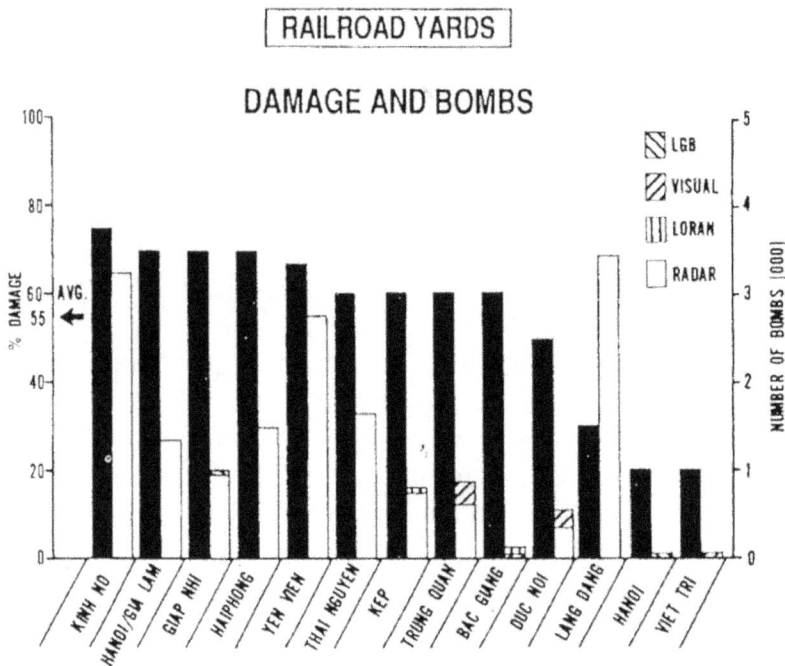

Figure 18

storage complexes associated with key rail yards were destroyed by the heavy attacks, thus greatly reducing the amount of covered storage capacity. Previous Linebacker I strikes, however, had forced a shift from rail to road traffic which probably caused the low stockpile levels found at these rail storage areas. This low level of stockpiles is the reason for the limited bomb damage visible to supplies in poststrike photography. The Linebacker II campaign would have been more effectively waged prior to Linebacker I when the rail-centered transportation network offered lucrative supply concentrations instead of the dispersed, truck-oriented system actually found during Linebacker II.

B-52s proved very successful against larger rail targets and fully achieved Strategic Air Command's (SAC) damage predictions at Yen Vien, Thai Nguyen, Haiphong, and most of the large Kinh No complex. They also made a significant contribution to the overall damage level achieved at the smaller rail yards of Giap Nhi, Kep, Duc Noi, and Trung Quan. F-4s and A-7s using visual techniques also were effective in attacks on these smaller rail yards, and F-4 laser strikes against the Hanoi railroad and classification yard clearly demonstrated the capability of terminally guided ordnance against area targets with critical strike restrictions. In the latter case, F-4s with eight laser guided bombs achieved a 20-percent damage level at a large rail facility through careful ordnance placement. The F-111 strike effort against this category of target was light, but some damage was achieved against all of the F-111 targets providing a definite military impact in addition to the obvious psychological and harassment effect.

Destruction of rail-related targets, probably the most significant achievement of Linebacker II, caused a complete disruption of rail traffic within 10 miles of Hanoi and a serious degradation of traffic on the northeast rail line and the internal loop. In addition to this military impact, the massive destruction resulting from the large number of weapons expended against these targets near Hanoi probably had a serious psychological effect on Hanoi's population.

Storage Facilities

The target category that received the second largest weight of effort was storage facilities. The 14 targets, varying from permanent warehouse complexes to open transshipment points, accounted for 25 percent of the Air Force effort. Three hundred thirty-nine strike sorties against these targets, delivered more than 12,000 bombs. On three targets, photo interpreters could not distinguish Linebacker II damage from that of Linebacker I strikes, and results are classified as unknown.

Reference to figure 19 indicates that most damage was caused by B-52s with the level of damage highly correlated with the weight of effort applied against the target. This relationship is even more apparent in figure 20 which compares damage with the number of bombs delivered on each target. (The correlation coefficient between percent damage and number of radar bombs is .73.) Apparently if satisfactory damage levels are to be achieved against storage areas, significant numbers of bombs must be expended, which implies employment of B-52s or large numbers of fighter-attack aircraft. During Linebacker I, LGBs were used extensively against storage area targets in sensitive

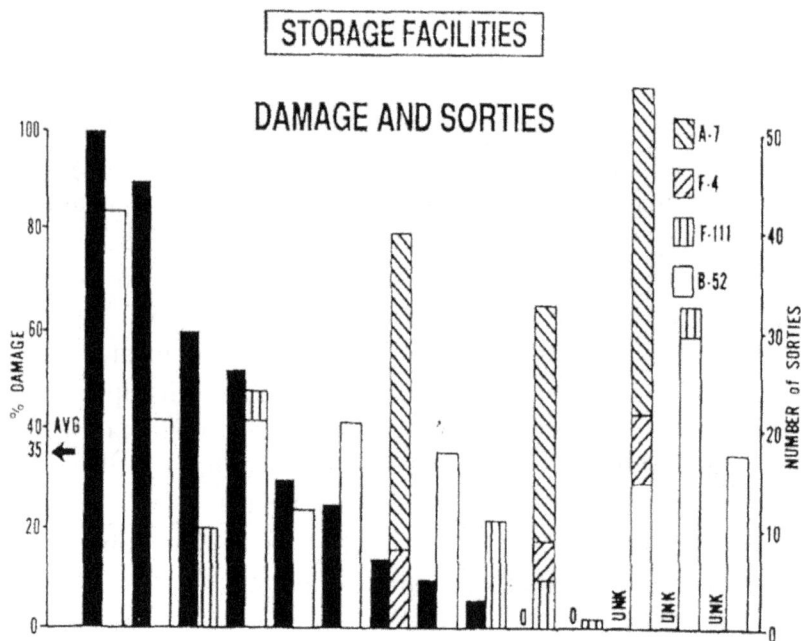

Figure 19

areas. While this tactic tended to preclude inadvertent damage to adjacent areas, it did not allow the desired damage level to be reached. In Linebacker II, large strike forces were employed against storage facilities and satisfactory damage levels were accomplished.

A notable exception was the destruction credited to F-111 aircraft at the Hanoi/Bac Mai airfield storage facility where 10 F-111 sorties effected a damage level of 60 percent. F-111s were also successful in keeping pressure on the enemy in areas where significant damage had already been attained by other weapons systems. F-4s and A-7s accomplished satisfactory damage levels when delivering ordnance visually; however, LORAN Pathfinder results were disappointing.

The lowest damage levels attained in this target category corresponded to transshipment points. Two received no damage, and on a third (Bac Giang), damage was unknown. Such targets should be carefully reviewed for lucrativeness before being struck. Effectiveness of large strike forces employed against transshipment points with little

82

or no fixed facilities is dependent upon the amount of open storage present. Continued harassment by single aircraft using variable tactics combined with MK-36 seeding of the waterway, when practicable, would reduce the enemy's activity level to a minimum. Large strike forces could better be employed against targets with such fixed facilities as railroad yards and storage areas or against transshipment points with large amounts of open storage.

The military impact of the strikes against storage facilities was significant but not long range since the enemy had returned to open storage techniques and had dispersed critical items of materiel. The relatively high damage levels sustained by many of the storage facilities, however, would require extensive reconstruction and diversion of effort from other areas. In addition, a significant psychological impact on the North Vietnamese populace may have been attained by the high damage levels as well as the attacks on previously "off limits" targets and areas.

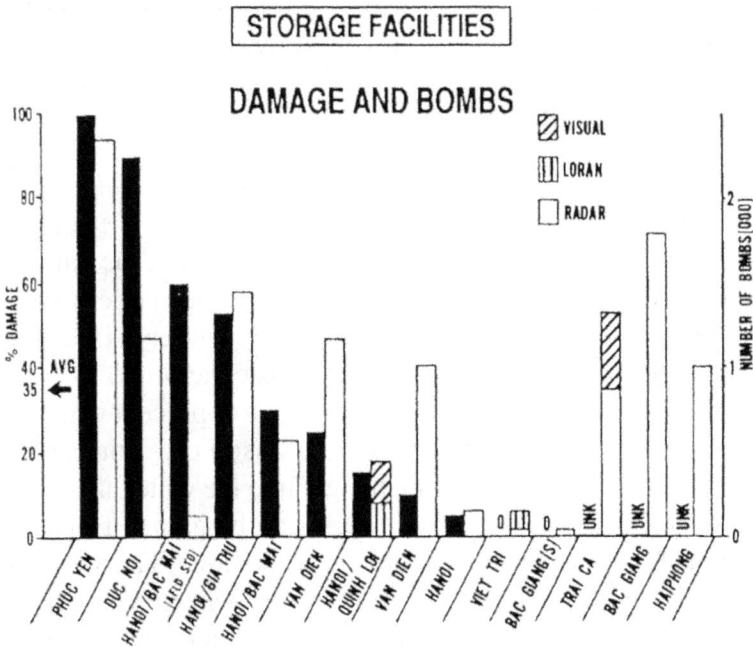

Figure 20

RADCOM FACILITIES

DAMAGE AND SORTIES

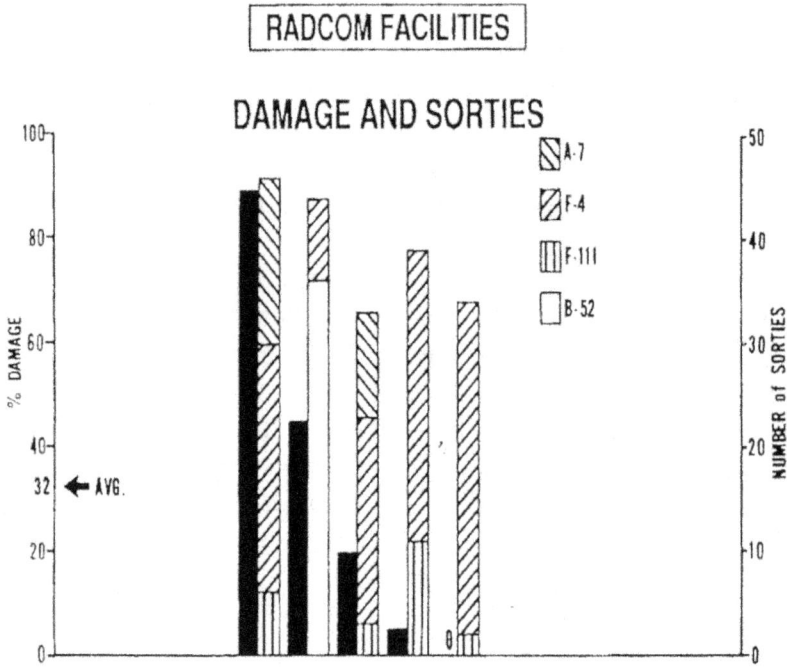

Figure 21

Radio Communications Facilities

The area type targets (railroad yards and storage facilities) discussed so far received 61 percent of the total sortie weight of effort. Turning now to what might be characterized as point targets, the category first in line is radio communications facilities. Five such targets were struck with 14 percent of the sortie effort. One hundred ninety-six strike sorties dropped approximately 3,600 bombs on these facilities.

Damage to radcom targets ranged from 90 to 0 percent with an overall average per target of 32 percent. A comparison of sorties and percent damage in figure 21 provides little insight into the wide range of damage level achieved, but considerable insight can be gained from figure 22 when damage is compared to the delivery technique. The higher damage levels on the left correspond to the employment of visually released general-purpose bombs and LGBs. The low damage levels on the right correspond to a higher percentage of LORAN deliveries. No bomb impacts from LORAN strikes could be found in the target areas.

B-52 and F-111 strikes were generally in the target area, but due to the nature of the targets, only limited damage was attained. Radcom facilities have a single essential element, the transmitter and receiver control building, which is generally protected by a concrete blast wall. A direct hit on the building is usually required to destroy it. Therefore, the most effective ordnance proved to be MK-84 LGBs.

The least lucrative military target system on the Linebacker II list was North Vietnamese radio communications facilities. With the exception of the virtual destruction of the Hanoi international radcom transmitter #2, the main effect of the strikes was a few brief periods of interrupted operations. The strikes also caused some frequency drifting and unscheduled changes and reductions in both domestic and international broadcasting and in long-distance military and civil radio communications. The redundancy in radcom facilities, however, allowed the North Vietnamese to maintain all necessary operations. The five transmitter and receiver stations targeted during Linebacker II were

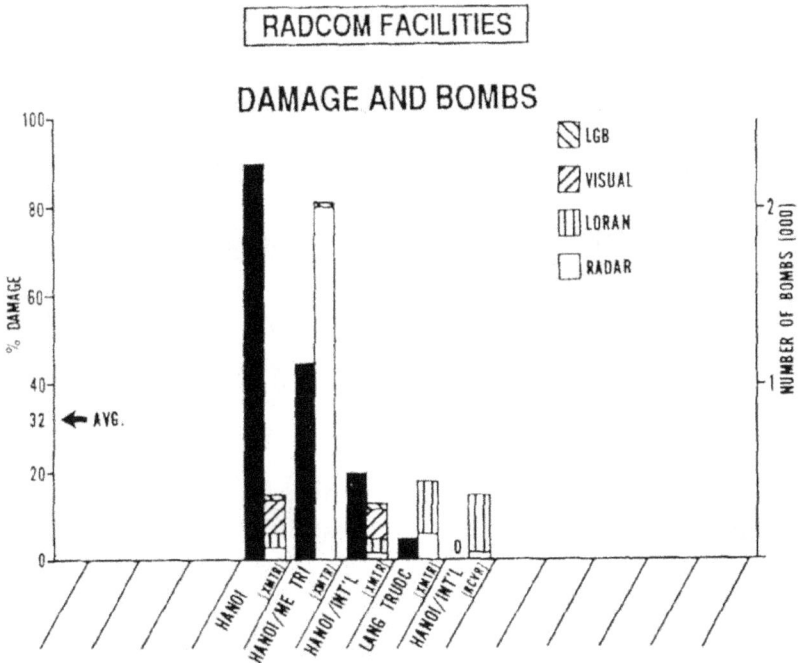

Figure 22

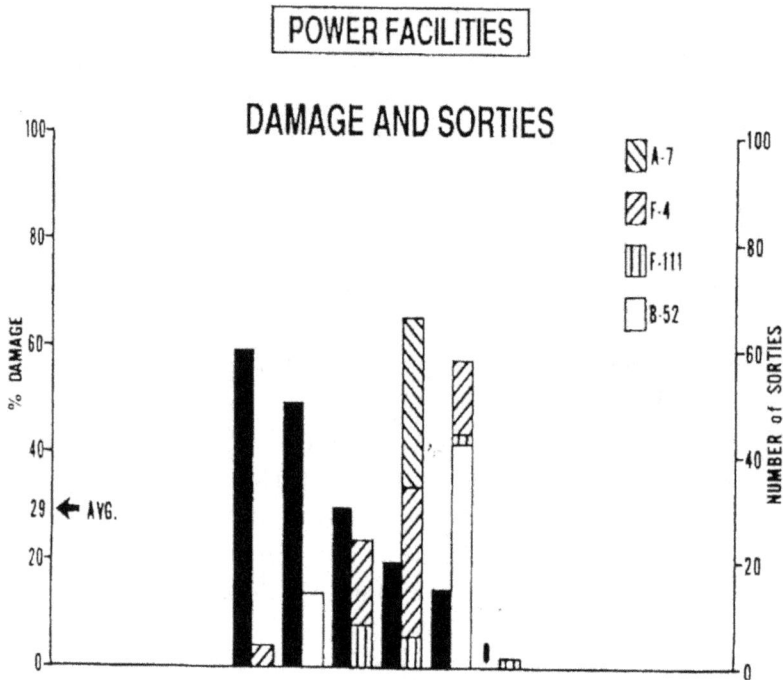

POWER FACILITIES

DAMAGE AND SORTIES

Figure 23

primary facilities; but, without complete destruction of all five (and their own alternate facilities), as well as serious damage to other, smaller transmitter and receiver stations, the impact was minimal. Some 14 percent of the total strike effort was expended against the radcom facilities, but poststrike analysis indicated that little of military value was achieved by the strikes. In addition, the strikes' psychological impact was questionable.

Power Facilities

Next in line is the category of electric power facilities including thermal power plants and transformer stations. The six targets in this category received 12 percent of the sortie effort (166 sorties delivered approximately 4,000 bombs).

Reference to figure 23 might lead one to believe that an inverse relationship exists between damage and the number of sorties striking a target, so again we must look to the delivery technique on figure 24.

The most significant damage to the North Vietnamese electric power system was accomplished by four F-4s using MK-84 laser guided bombs against the Hanoi thermal power plant. This key power plant was rendered nonoperational resulting in disruption of power to the capital city. The North Vietnamese needed at least six months to repair this facility.

Although there are indications of some damage to the Haiphong and Hanoi transformer stations from radar and LORAN bomb deliveries, the LGB proved to be the most effective munition against power facility targets. Terminally guided ordnance should be used against the critical elements of power facilities; unguided ordnance provides too small a probability of damage per sortie and the weight of effort would be better used against area targets.

An air campaign against the electric power system of a country should not have as an objective the total cutoff of power. All critical elements of military and governmental agencies have alternate means of

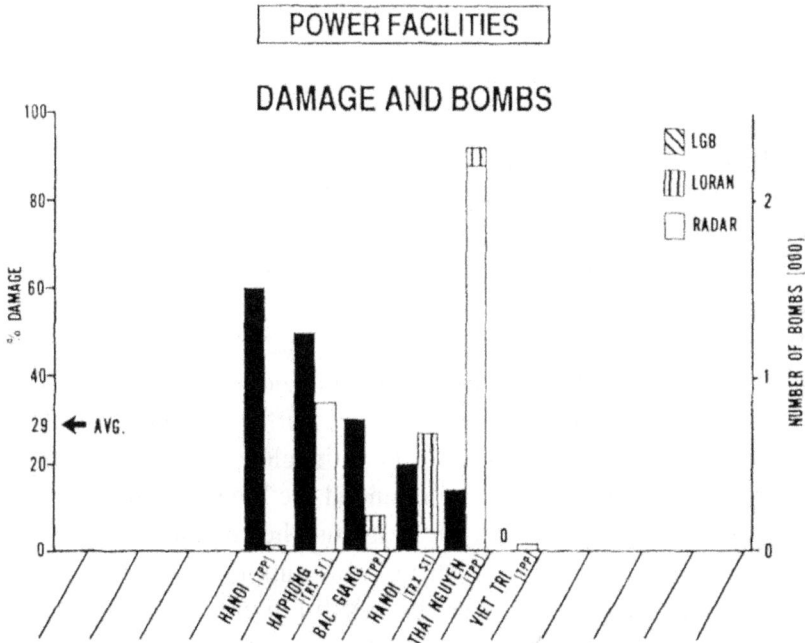

POWER FACILITIES

DAMAGE AND BOMBS

Figure 24

generating electric power. However, if the goals of an air campaign are to disrupt and harass military and governmental agencies and psychologically affect the common man, attacks on the electric power system should be considered. When it is possible to strike all power plants serving an area, the power plants should receive the emphasis. Strikes on transformer stations cause the enemy to construct bypass methods of transmission and degrade quality of electric power but will not stop transmission of unregulated power to consumers.

The military impact of Linebacker II strikes on power facilities, together with previous damages, was significant since Hanoi's major sources of power were, for the first time, nonoperable. At the start of Linebacker II, approximately half of the national power capacity of 230,000 kilowatts was operational. Attacks on the power system limited the maximum power capability available to the Hanoi and Haiphong industrial complex to approximately 29,000 kilowatts. The limited amount of power available was probably supplied only to such priority users as the more important industrial installations, foreign embassies, and selected government buildings in Hanoi.

Airfields

The fifth target category is enemy airfields. The Air Force targeted a total of five airfields during Linebacker II, and an additional airfield, Gia Lam, was accidently damaged by nearby strikes. Ten percent of the sortie effort was applied against these targets (141 strike sorties delivered approximately 2,200 bombs).

The most obvious result reflected on figures 25 and 26 is the low level of damage caused by the strikes against airfields. Four of the airfields experienced 10 percent damage and one suffered 5 percent, for an overall average of only 9 percent. The airfield receiving the highest percentage of LORAN strikes experienced the lowest damage level.

The most effective weapon system against the airfields was the B-52. The primary intention of B-52 strikes was suppressing MiG activity, and in all cases these strikes were successful in cratering the runways. F-4 and A-7 all-weather success is probably best measured at Yen Bai Airfield where the 44 fighter-bombers constituted the major strike force.

The airfield was not seriously damaged by the F-4 and A-7 strikes that involved LORAN delivery techniques. The only reported period of nonoperational status at Yen Bai resulted from a successful F-111 sortie.

Despite the weight of effort employed against airfields during both Linebacker I and II, jet-capable runways were not sufficiently interdicted at any one airfield in North Vietnam to prevent air operations. Even the most effective strikes proved capable only of hindering operations for a short while, and PACAF did not recommend airfields for inclusion in target lists for strikes in North Vietnam. LORAN delivery techniques offered only a limited probability of damage to airfield facilities, while F-111s, used in limited numbers, proved to be primarily a harassment weapon system. To maximize harassment, however, incendiary and fragmentation cluster bomb munitions should have been considered.

Measuring military impact by BDA, the Linebacker II strikes against airfields were only a limited success since the already damaged airfields offered few lucrative facilities and little long-term damage was

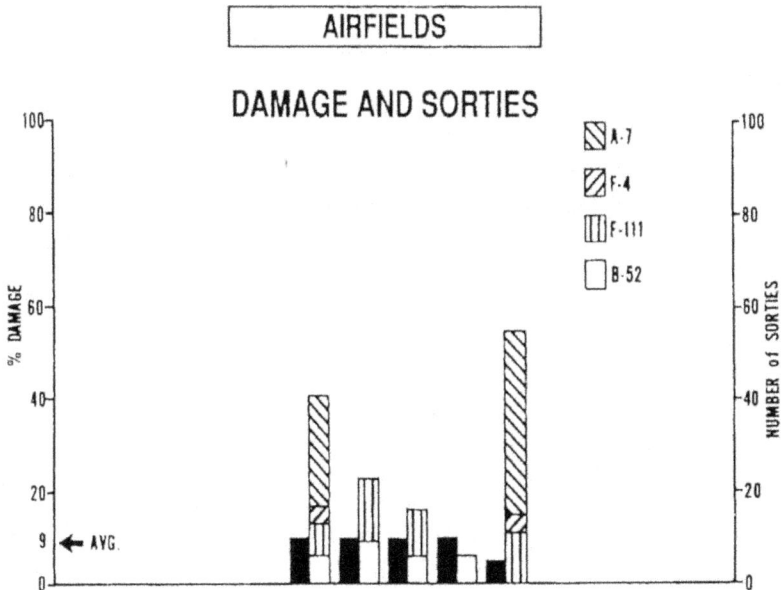

Figure 25

| AIRFIELDS |

DAMAGE AND BOMBS

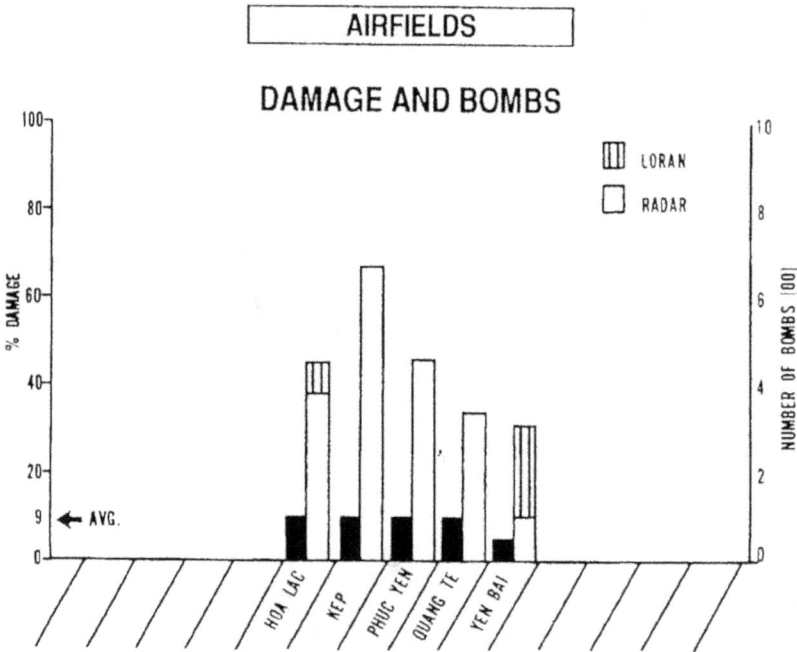

Figure 26

achieved. The runway cratering, however, probably succeeded in hindering MiG flight operations and may have contributed to the low MiG engagement record during Linebacker II. F-111 strikes during nighttime hours contributed an immeasurable psychological effect by harassing nighttime repair efforts.

Surface-to-Air Missile Sites

The Air Force struck 13 SAM sites during Linebacker II with 2 percent of the sortie effort. Twenty-nine strike sorties delivered approximately 1,300 bombs, mostly in a prestrike suppression role.

All strikes against SAM sites were conducted by B-52 and F-111 aircraft using radar delivery techniques (figs. 27 and 28). Two sites suffered 50 percent damage, one struck by B-52s and the other by F-111s. At eight sites, photo interpreters noted no damage, and at three others, the percentage of damage is unknown because there were no poststrike photos. The average damage level, based on the 10 sites with known results, was 10 percent, the second lowest of all target categories.

Historically the North Vietnamese had demonstrated an ability to relocate SAM sites rapidly. They could accomplish this feat in approximately four hours. Target selection against easily movable targets is critical and should be accomplished only after an exhaustive examination of all-source intelligence. Further, unless the time interval between confirmation of occupied status and the strike is less than four hours, there can be no assurance that the targeted elements will be in the designated area. When the time interval is in terms of days or weeks, there exists a high probability that the sites will not be occupied at the time of strike. During the Linebacker II campaign, two of the 13 sites attacked were reported as being unoccupied at the time of the attack.

In considering strikes against SAM sites in terms of target vulnerability and weapon selection, two facts are apparent. The first is that at a SAM site the most vulnerable component is the revetted or unrevetted guidance radar. Second, if the objective of the attack is to

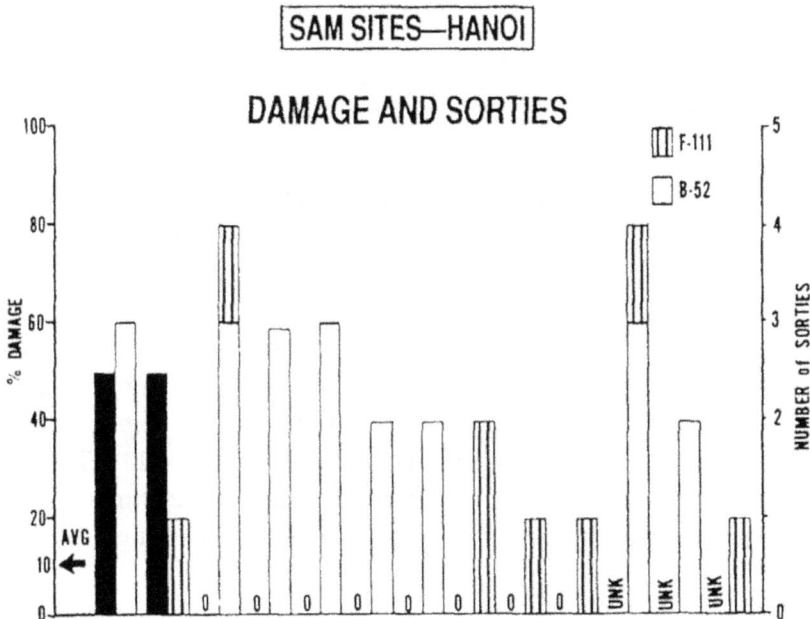

SAM SITES—HANOI

DAMAGE AND SORTIES

Figure 27

SAM SITES—HANOI

DAMAGE AND BOMBS

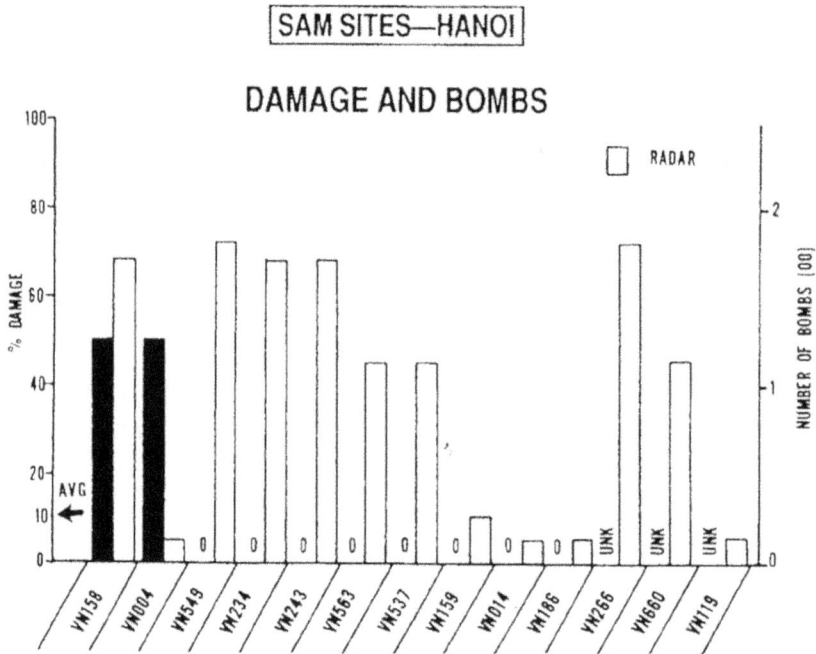

Figure 28

suppress rather than destroy the site, the optimum weapon for achieving this objective should be selected. During the Linebacker II campaign, aim points for all fighter-attack strikes against all sites were properly selected; however, all strikes, including B-52s, released iron bombs which afforded the least chance of damaging the site. Unless large numbers of strike aircraft delivering iron bombs are used, only minimum damage should be expected. Actual results indicate that only two of the sites received damage. PACAF weaponeering indicates that a significantly higher damage level could have been expected had the CBU-52 cluster bomb munition been employed (table 11). The lack of accurate and complete information precludes determination of the military and psychological impact of strikes on SAM sites.

Table 11

SAM Site Weaponeering

Weapons System	Type Damage*	Weapon	PD Per Sortie**	Sorties Required for 50% PD
B-52	K-Kill	108 MK-82	0.3%	211
B-52	F-Kill	· 66 CBU-52	15.9%	4
F-111	K-Kill	12 MK-82	0.5%	148
F-111	F-Kill	12 CBU-52	62.9%	1

*K-Kill: Destruction of site.

 F-Kill: Damage which renders site inoperative for at least two hours.

**PD: Probability of damage.

Bridges

The final target category is bridges. As a category, bridges received less than 1 percent of the Air Force sortie effort during Linebacker II, illustrating the change in objectives away from interdiction. Only three bridges were struck by nine F-111 and F-4 sorties delivering 68 bombs.

Of the three bridges struck, one was completely interdicted and the other two suffered no significant damage. All damage resulted from F-4s delivering LGBs on the Hanoi railroad and highway bridge over the Canal des Rapides (figs. 29 and 30). Damage to this bridge disrupted all rail traffic on the northeast and northwest rail lines, but the North Vietnamese initiated immediate repairs to minimize the disruption. F-111s were generally ineffective in interdicting bridges although at the Lang Lau railroad bridge, new craters were observed on both sides of the river. The overall damage assessment of 33 percent is rather tenuous due to the small sample upon which it is based. It is obvious, however, from this and previous campaigns that LGBs provide the best results against bridge targets. This means that any effective campaign against bridges requires good operational weather.

BRIDGES

DAMAGE AND SORTIES

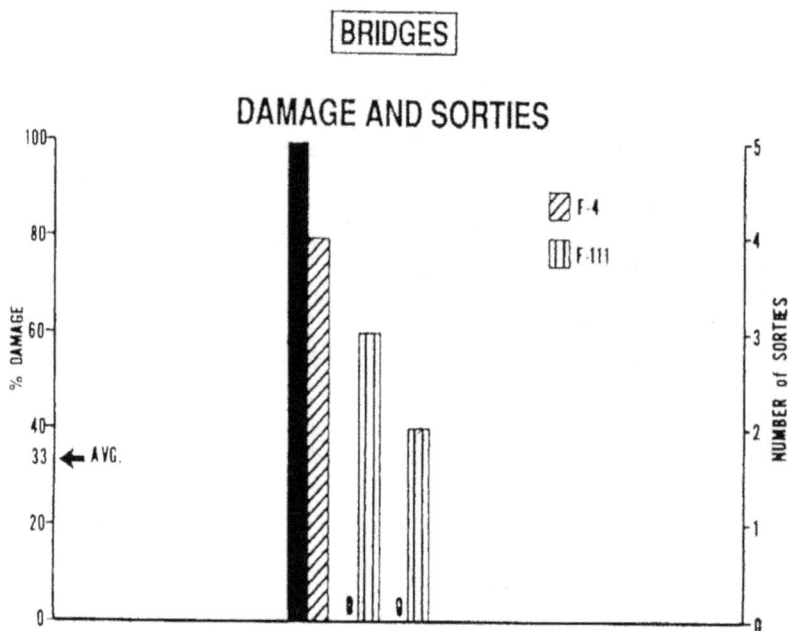

Figure 29

To disrupt rail traffic in a long-term campaign, a few key bridges should be struck to isolate the traffic, then a large-scale effort against major rail yards and sidings to destroy available rolling stock and locomotives should follow. After these initial strikes, a balanced effort between bridges and rail yards provides the best means of disrupting the rail traffic. The military effect of the strikes on bridges during the short Linebacker II campaign, however, was limited to the temporary disruption of rail and road traffic over the Canal des Rapides. Any psychological impact resulting from the strikes was probably minor.

Damage Summary

Table 12 summarizes the average strike effort and damage results against the seven target categories just discussed. Target categories are listed in order of the total strike effort applied against each.

BRIDGES

DAMAGE AND BOMBS

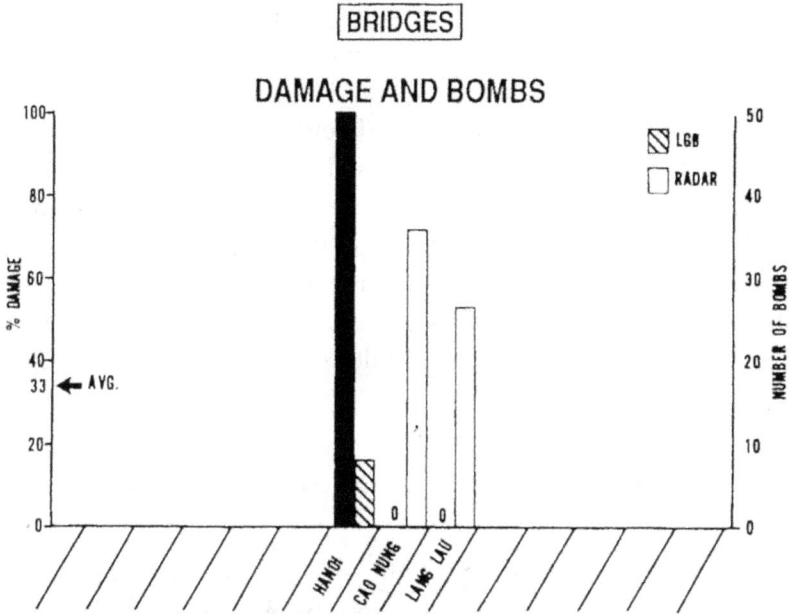

Figure 30

Table 12

Strike Effort and Damage Summary

Target Category	Targets Struck	Sorties Per Target	Bombs Per Target	Damage Per Target (%)
Railroad Yards	13	37	1,421	55
Storage Facilities	14	24	890	35
Radcom Facilities	5	39	720	32
Power Facilities	6	28	666	29
Airfields	5	28	446	9
SAM Sites	13	2	98	10
Bridges	3	3	23	33
Overall	59	23	713	32

The highest average number of sorties per target was flown against railroad yards and radcom facilities and the lowest against SAM sites and bridges. By far the greatest number of bombs per target was expended against railroad yards, reflecting the intense B-52 effort against that target category. The highest damage level was also achieved against railroad yards, followed by storage facilities, bridges, radcom, and power facilities. The lowest levels of damage were achieved against airfields and SAM sites. Overall damage for the campaign weighted by the number of targets struck in each category was 32 percent. This damage level was achieved in just 11 days that were virtually dominated by bad weather.

Release System Accuracy and Employment

Additional insight into bombing effectiveness can be gained if damage statistics are analyzed by release system. On the 53 targets with known results, some 37,680 bombs were dropped. A large majority, 90.7 percent, of the bombs were released with radar and another 6.5 percent with LORAN, both all-weather systems. Only about 3 percent were dropped under conditions that permitted visual or laser guidance deliveries.

Since most targets were struck with bombs released from more than one type system, regression analysis was used to estimate the individual contribution of each. A simple linear model of the following form was employed:

$$Y = \alpha + \Sigma B_i X_i$$

where:
Y = Percent damage to the target
α = Constant term
B_i = Regression coefficient or marginal product of one bomb from system i
X_i = Number of bombs released with system i

The estimated regression equation and summary statistics are given below:

		T-ratio
Percent Damage = 18.136		
− .028 (LORAN bombs)		.83
+ .016 (Radar bombs)		3.88
+ .123 (Visual bombs)		1.80
+ 2.007 (LG bombs)		1.68

$R^2 = .33$

This linear equation explains 33 percent of the variation in damage on the 53 targets with known results. With the exception of LORAN deliveries, the contribution of bombs released under each system is significant at the 95 percent confidence level using a one-tail T test. The partial correlation for LORAN deliveries is negative, but the T test is so weak we cannot reject the null hypothesis that no relationship exists between target damage and the number of bombs released. Even the incorporation of qualitative variables in the equation to distinguish target categories did not alter this result.

Table 13 summarizes the results discussed above with the regression coefficients entered in the second row. Based on the analysis, the contribution or marginal product of LORAN bombing is assumed to be zero. In other words, it appears that LORAN bombing made no significant contribution to the overall damage level during Linebacker II. Assessments pertaining to the effectiveness of LORAN bombing on individual targets have been discussed previously. This statistical evaluation lends support to those assessments. The LORAN strikes, deep into North Vietnam, were made at the fringe of reliable reception in an area in which there had been only limited previous reconnaissance for target coordinate calibration. Under these conditions, LORAN bombing does not appear to have been effective.

Setting radar effectiveness at a normalized factor of one in the third row, the coefficients in the second row indicate that a visually released conventional bomb was roughly about eight times more effective and an LGB about 124 times more effective than a radar-released bomb.

This would make an LGB about 16 times more effective than a visually released conventional bomb.

Table 13

Release System Summary

	LORAN	Radar	Visual	Laser
Percent of Total Bombs Released	6.5	90.7	2.6	.2
Marginal Product of One Bomb (% increase in damage)	.000	.016	.123	2.007
Relative Effectiveness Factor	—	1	8	124

A more accurate estimate of the effectiveness of both radar and laser guided bombing can be gained if the data are fitted with curvilinear rather than the linear relationships used for the comparison in table 13. As an example, the following estimated equation shows the increased statistical power that results when nonlinear functions for radar and LGB bombing are used:

T-ratio

Percent Damage $= 9.800$

$+ \ 3.897 \ (100\text{s of radar bombs})$ 4.84

$- \ .002 \ (100\text{s of radar bombs})^3$ 2.80

$+ \ 8.382 \ (\text{LG bombs})$ 4.12

$- \ .038 \ (\text{LG bombs})^3$ 3.38

$R^2 = .45$

Forty-five percent of the variation in damage is now explained, and the T ratios imply a much higher level of statistical confidence in the individual relationships.

A graphical comparison of the difference in LGB and radar effectiveness implied by the two regression equations is presented in figure 31. The linear fits are relatively flat because the lines are forced through points to the right of the graphs, results achieved when more than 2,500 radar bombs or eight LGBs were expended on a target. The

RADAR AND LGB BOMBING EFFECTIVENESS

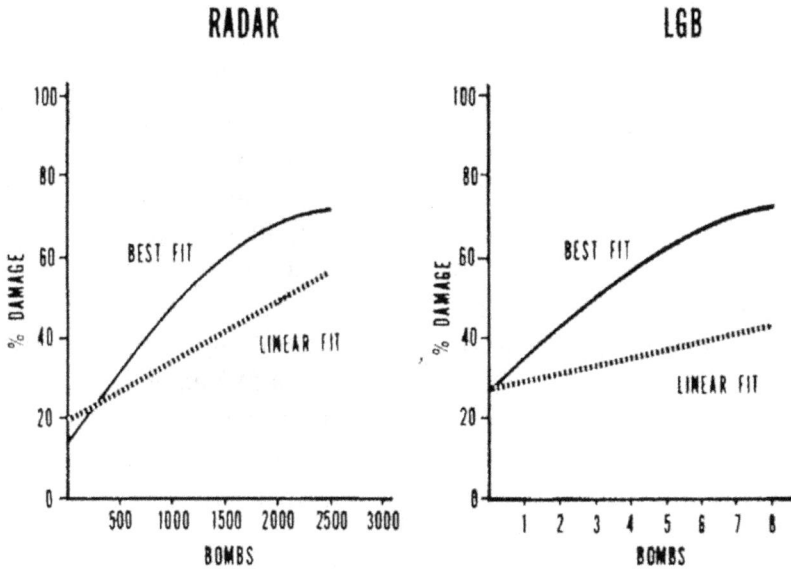

RADAR

LGB

Figure 31

lines that best fit the data rise more sharply and then level off after these values. For the targets struck during Linebacker II, it appears that little additional damage was gained when expenditures were increased above these levels. Fortunately, this occurred on only four targets. If we confine ourselves to the more effective ranges, radar bombing was about two times more effective and laser guided bombing three times more effective than depicted on the comparison given in table 13.

The above effectiveness comparisons have been made on an individual bomb basis. To convert these statistics to a per sortie basis, the bomb load carried by a sortie must be considered. As an example, using bomb loads of 12 conventional MK-82s or two MK-84 LGBs, the comparison in table 13 equates to about a 3:1 effectiveness ratio between LGB and visual conventional bomb sorties. The more effective LGB range depicted in figure 31, however, implies a 9:1 ratio. This 3:1 to 9:1 effectiveness range corresponds closely to that computed in other studies of strikes on such individual targets as tanks, trucks, bridges, antiaircraft guns, and interdiction points.

Weather Constraints and Implications

The results outlined above, namely the relative ineffectiveness of LORAN bombing and the high effectiveness of laser guided bombing, should be carefully weighed in programming future bombing campaigns. As an example, figure 32 graphs the total number of strike sorties flown during Linebacker II by their times over target (TOT) during the day. A vast majority of the daytime effort was conducted between 1200 and 1500. This timing leads to possible criticism of stereotyped operations; however, rationale can be provided for such a profile. If the expected value of LORAN bombing is zero, or very low, while laser guided bombing has a strong positive expected value, then within limitations, it makes sense to employ the force during the time of day when the probability of weather favorable to LGB operations is highest.

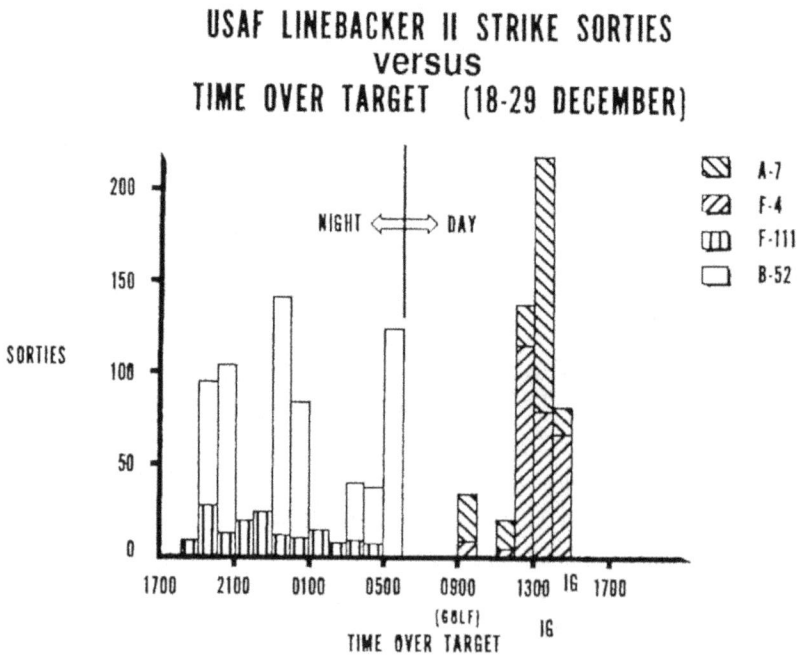

USAF LINEBACKER II STRIKE SORTIES versus
TIME OVER TARGET (18-29 DECEMBER)

Figure 32

WEATHER EFFECTS
TACAIR
HANOI-HAIPHONG/RP-6
(18-29 DECEMBER 1972)

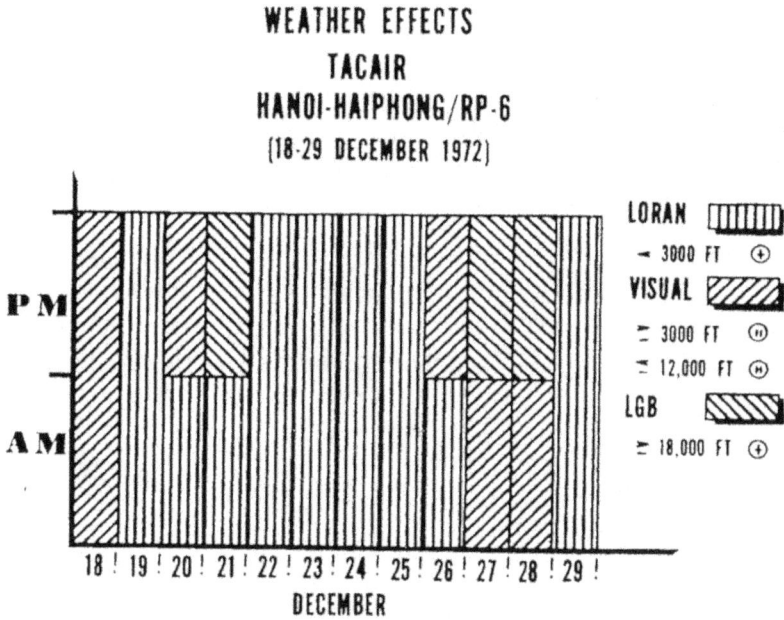

Figure 33

Figures 33 and 34 indicate that this is what occurred. Figure 33 shows that weather favorable to visual, and particularly to LGB operations, occurred during the afternoon periods. In general, however, weather was unfavorable throughout the campaign with weather windows occurring only on the afternoons of 21, 27, and 28 December. Figure 34 shows that visual and LGB deliveries were made on these dates but that there was no apparent effort to surge and take advantage of the brief periods of favorable weather. There are, of course, reasons that the surge did not occur. LGB pods were in short supply and the requirement to support late-night B-52 strikes limited the options for generating additional daytime sorties. Nevertheless, these are lessons learned from Linebacker II that should be considered during the planning stage of future air campaigns. First, we still require an improved tactical aircraft all-weather bombing capability. In the meantime, we should investigate ways to improve surge capability to take better advantage of periods of favorable weather.

Actual versus Predicted Target Damage

Perhaps the most valid way to evaluate the bombing effectiveness of a campaign is to compare actual accomplishments against what one might reasonably expect to accomplish given the resources available. To determine predicted damage values, Pacific Air Forces weaponeers, using SAC B-52 damage estimates and the standard fighter-attack release parameters of table 14 for the actual number of bombs delivered, computed the cumulative damage expected for total strikes against each Linebacker II target.[5] The comparative results are presented in the next section.

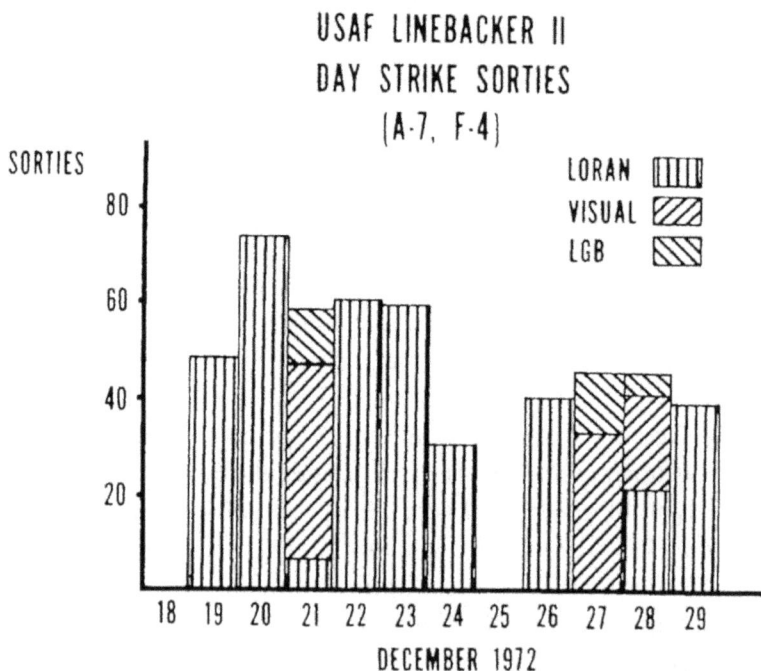

USAF LINEBACKER II
DAY STRIKE SORTIES
(A-7, F-4)

Figure 34

Table 14

Standard Release Parameters

Release Parameter	B-52 Radar	F-111 Radar	F-4 Visual	A-7 Visual	F-4 LGB	A-11 LORAN
Altitude (feet)	37,000	500	7,000	7,000	14,000	17,000
Dive Angle	0°	0°	45°	45°	45°	0°
Knots True Airspeed	470	480	500	500	500	500
Circular Error Probability (feet)	1,250	500	483	111	20	984

Comparisons by Target Category

Figures 35 through 41 present scatter diagrams for actual versus predicted target damage. Percent actual damage is measured on the vertical axis and percent predicted damage on the horizontal axis. Each point designates an individual target. The 45° line through the origin is the locus of points where actual and predicted damage are equal. If a point falls above this line, actual damage was above that predicted; conversely, if the point falls below the line, actual damage was less than predicted. The light line is a regression line through the major scatter of points and indicates the general relationship between actual and predicted damage. Points designated with a triangle lie outside the general pattern described by the other points.

Directing attention first to railroad yards (fig. 35), we see that on about half the targets actual damage was above that predicted, and on the other half damage was below that predicted. The regression line indicates that in the lower prediction ranges, actual damage was greater than expected while in the higher ranges actual damage fell slightly below that expected. The outlying point designated by the triangle is Lang Dang railroad yard. The effort and results at this target were outlined in a previous section.

For storage facilities (fig. 36), eight of the 11 known damage points fell below the 45° line in the general pattern shown by the light line. On three occasions, however, actual damage was well above that predicted. The left triangle depicts results of the very successful F-111 strike against the Hanoi/Bac Mai airfield storage facility. The other two are

LINEBACKER II

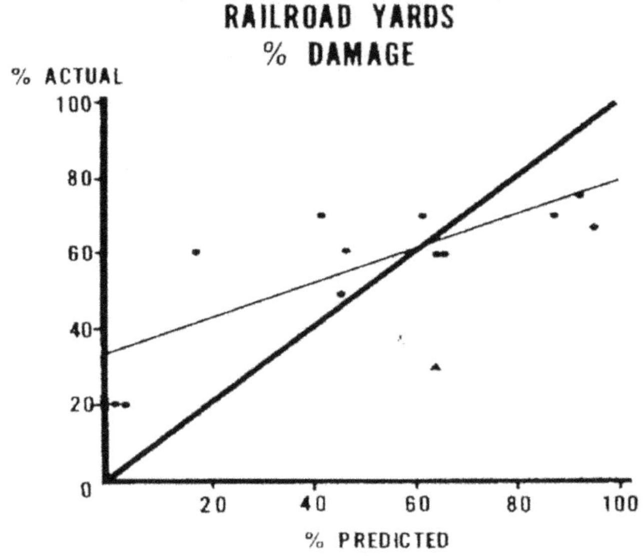

RAILROAD YARDS
% DAMAGE

Figure 35

B-52 strikes against the Phuc Yen SAM support area and the Duc Noi warehouse complex. Both were well defined, highly tangible targets.

Comparative results for strikes against radio communications and power facilities are shown on figures 37 and 38 and follow the general patterns depicted by the light lines. Damage results for these two categories generally fell below that predicted except for the LGB strike against the Hanoi radcom transmitter #2 and the B-52 effort against the Haiphong transformer station. The highest percentage of destruction against power facilities (60 percent), however, resulted from an LGB strike against the Hanoi thermal power plant, the highest point on the right of the graph.

Figure 39 shows that damage to airfields was well below that expected. On four targets more than 70 percent damage was predicted, but only 10 percent was realized. This result could mean that the airfield predictions were overly optimistic. For SAM sites (fig. 40) very little damage was predicted and, in eight of 10 cases, little was achieved. Only three bridges were struck (fig. 41); and for two out of the three, little damage was predicted or achieved. The one bridge totally interdicted was struck with laser guided ordnance.

Summary Comparison

Figure 42 summarizes the average actual and predicted damage statistics by target category. The highest and most accurately predicted damage of Linebacker II resulted from strikes against railroad yards. Next in line by level of damage came storage facilities, bridges, radcom facilities, and power facilities. Average bridge damage was higher than predicted, and this result can be attributed to the one highly successful LGB strike. Conversely, average damage to radcom facilities was only about one-half that predicted. Lying well below the other categories with respect to average damage results were strikes against the enemy's defensive installations, SAM sites, and airfields. Average damage to SAM sites was above that predicted, and this outcome can be attributed wholly to attacks on two sites where 50 percent damage was achieved. Average damage to airfields was not only low but also was well beneath the predicted level.

LINEBACKER II

STORAGE FACILITIES
% DAMAGE

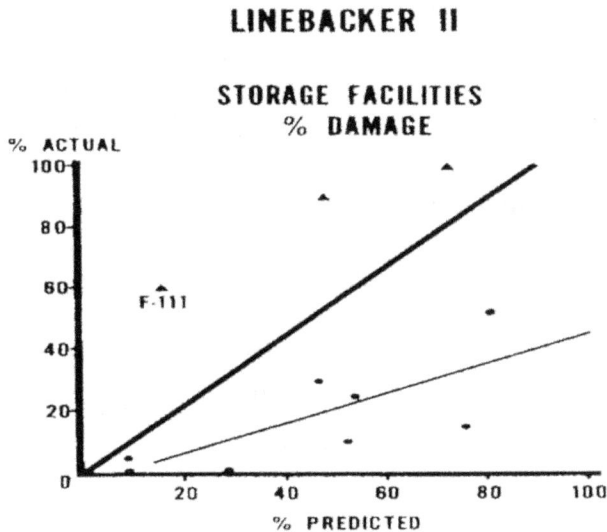

Figure 36

LINEBACKER II

RADCOM FACILITIES
% DAMAGE

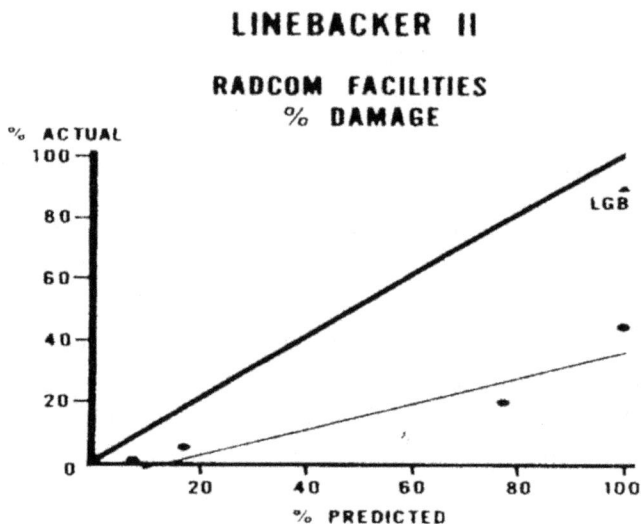

Figure 37

Overall actual damage weighted by the number of targets in each category was 32 percent (table 15). The comparable predicted damage was 40 percent. In other words, approximately 80 percent of the physical damage that weaponeers estimated was possible with the air resources employed was actually achieved. Without a basis of comparison, it is difficult to assert whether this "actual-to-predicted" ratio is good or bad. However, if we consider that actual BDA is also a function of marginal and irregular weather, varying release parameters, and enemy defensive reactions, none of which are incorporated in weaponeering predictions, the 80 percent figure is probably quite acceptable, if not rather phenomenal.

Table 15

Actual versus Predicted Damage Summary

Target Category	Targets	Average Actual Damage (%)	Average Predicted Damage (%)
Railroad Yards	13	55	52
Storage Facilities	11	35	44
Radcom Facilities	5	32	60
Power Facilities	6	29	42
Airfields	5	9	66
SAM Sites	10	10	1
Bridges	3	33	14
Overall	53*	32	40

*Three storage-facility and three SAM-site targets with unknown damage not included.

Campaign Lessons

In addition to the specific findings already discussed, certain general lessons surfaced during Linebacker II that deserve consideration in future campaign planning. These lessons are discussed below.

An Expanded Target List

The Joint Chiefs of Staff selected and validated all targets for Linebacker II. Generally, the targets were the most lucrative and valuable targets in North Vietnam, and their selection was ideal for achieving the objectives of Linebacker II. A more expansive target list, however, would have provided the operational commander with more flexibility to overcome periods of target area congestion and poor weather. A target list should be comprehensive enough to satisfy both the campaign objective and the requirements for force flexibility during the stated duration of the strike effort. Such a target list would provide optional targets while analysis of poststrike photography and other sources of intelligence would be used to determine: (1) the percent of damage achieved, (2) requirements for follow-on strikes, (3) adjustments to the desired mean point of impact, and (4) enemy defense capabilities and force vulnerability.

Strikes against Enemy Defenses

When considering strikes against enemy defenses (airfields and SAM sites), the duration of the campaign is of prime importance. A campaign of short duration should not consider defenses as an active target type for other than a suppression or harassment objective. Acceptable damage levels require a large weight of effort, more than can be allocated in a short period of time if other targets are to be struck. During a long campaign, however, elimination of the defensive threat (if the enemy is defense-limited) will better enable the strike force to achieve

LINEBACKER II

POWER FACILITIES
% DAMAGE

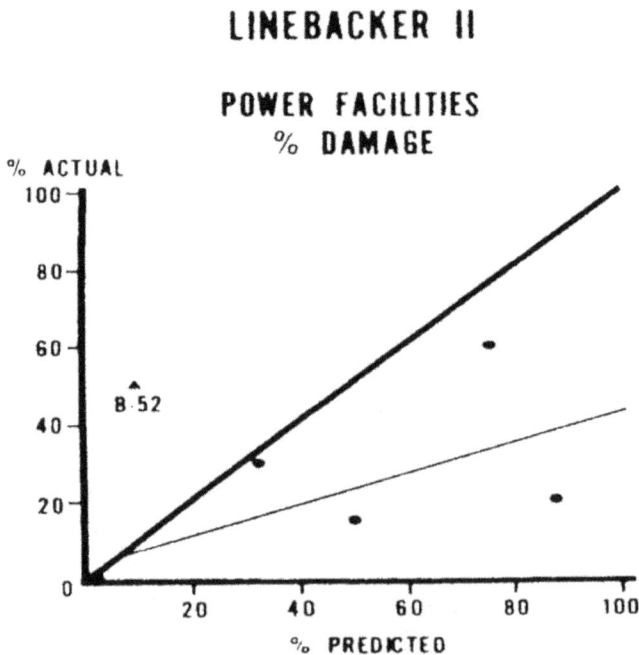

Figure 38

LINEBACKER II

AIRFIELDS
% DAMAGE

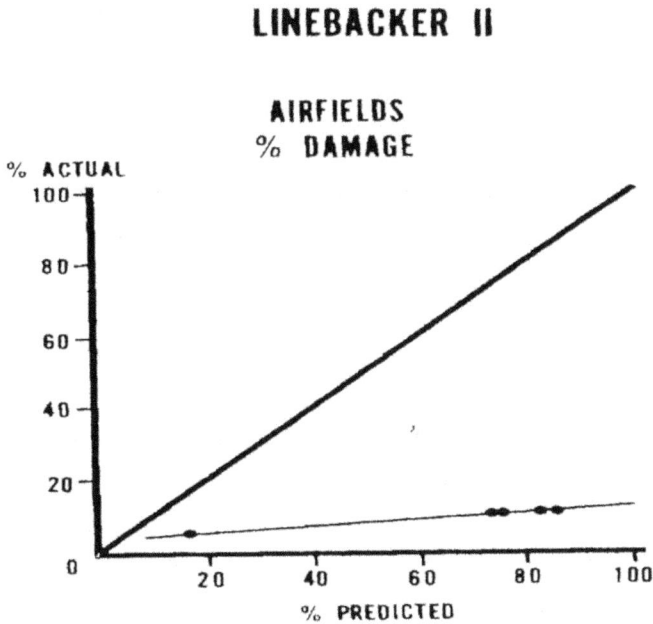

Figure 39

the campaign objectives. An early effort mounted against defenses in conjunction with strikes on other lucrative targets would enhance the continuing effort.

All-Weather Bombing Capability

Weaponeering and poststrike BDA analyses indicate that terminally guided ordnance, such as laser guided bombs, is most effective in achieving damage to targets with a single essential element. Such targets as the boilerhouse of a thermal power plant, the switch control building of a transformer station, the transmitter and receiver building of a radcom facility, or a bridge were significantly damaged only when LGBs were used. Operational weather was a major factor in the limited use of LGBs.

Strikes by B-52s or F-4s and A-7s using LORAN generally resulted in little damage to these pinpoint targets. F-111 effectiveness was limited by the use of single-ship flights with a small bomb load. In several cases, bombs were on target, but limitations in intervalometer settings on the F-111s prevented the destruction of the single essential target element.

In addition, analysis of LORAN strikes during Linebacker II indicates that even area-type targets were missed by a considerable distance. As a result, extensive research should be devoted to developing and refining an all-weather strike capability for use on the outer fringes of LORAN or in areas where no LORAN capability exists.

Strike Phasing

The damage achieved by the effort against the major North Vietnamese rail and storage facilities represented the most significant results of the campaign. Speculation on poststrike analysis indicates that the damage and disruption could have been even more significant if

LINEBACKER II

SAM SITES
% DAMAGE

LINEBACKER II

BRIDGES
% DAMAGE

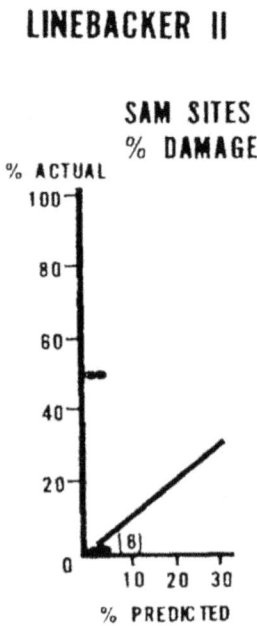

Figure 40

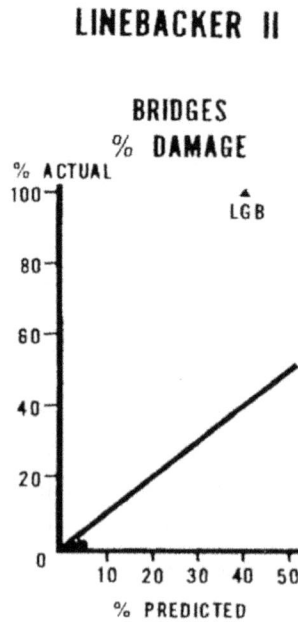

Figure 41

LINEBACKER II
PERCENT AVERAGE DAMAGE SUMMARY

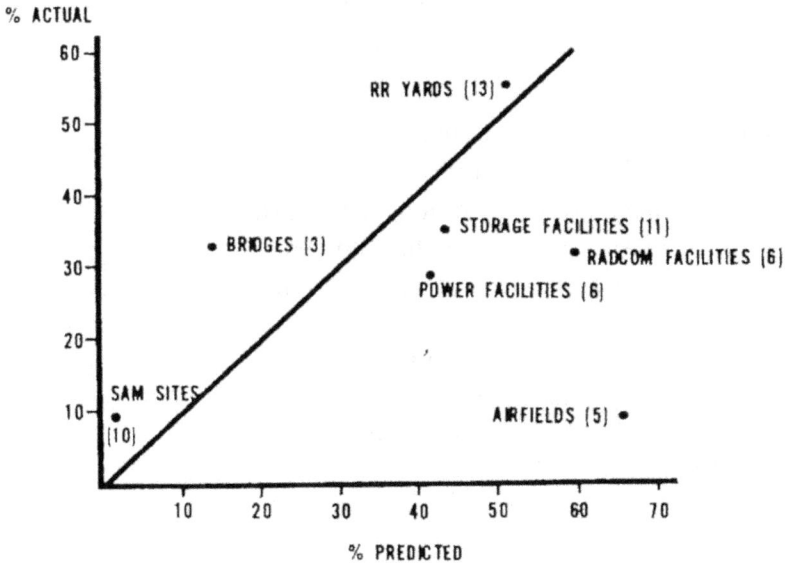

Figure 42

these same targets had been struck with the same concentrated effort at the start of Linebacker I (before the enemy shifted to truck movement and dispersed storage). Large-scale destruction of rail and storage facilities in the immediate Hanoi and Haiphong areas followed by the extensive interdiction campaign of Linebacker I would have undoubtedly hindered North Vietnamese resupply efforts far more effectively than the actual strategy promulgated. Because of the small force levels employed and the restrictive nature of Linebacker I operations, the North Vietnamese were able to make adjustments to maintain their vital supply lines. US efforts in Linebacker I seriously disrupted the North Vietnamese at first, but the development of a truck-oriented supply system for the heartland area, along with an expanded logistics system, made viable targeting extremely difficult. If the renewed strike effort in North Vietnam had commenced during a good weather period as Linebacker I did and had been concentrated like

Linebacker II, the end result might have been the isolation of North Vietnam from the outside supplies so vital to its war effort for a much longer period of time than that achieved.

Strike Patterns

Air Force aircraft encountered intense defensive reactions throughout Linebacker II. Nineteen aircraft were lost, including 15 B-52s. The primary threat to B-52 operations was surface-to-air SA-2 missiles. Some 1,000 SA-2s were launched against B-52s during the 12-day period. All the B-52s lost were targeted within a 10-nautical radius of Hanoi. Although the B-52 attrition rate of 2 percent did not appear exorbitant, it was still cause for alarm.

Nine B-52s were lost in the first three days. An immediate investigation revealed that during the first three nights of operations B-52 strikes followed recurring patterns. Three waves of aircraft struck targets each night at almost identical times. Timing between waves was similar from night to night, ingress and egress headings and altitudes for a given target were often identical, and the same posttarget turns were used. This repetitiousness allowed the North Vietnamese to anticipate our strike patterns and to salvo missiles in the target area with deadly results. The reason given for using standardized strike patterns was that they would be helpful to crews inexperienced in flying in such high-threat environments as Hanoi, but the use of such patterns was a costly mistake. After the third night in which six B-52s were lost, strike patterns were varied and the loss rate appreciably declined.[6]

Some writers attribute the lower attrition rate to their belief that North Vietnam's SAM supply had been destroyed or expended by the end of the campaign, but the data indicate otherwise. The number of SAMs sighted per B-52 sortie increased from 1.2 during the first phase of the campaign to 1.9 during the last phase.[7] As a previous section indicated, strikes against SAM sites were not particularly lucrative. A more reasonable answer to the decline in attrition would be the change in US tactics after the third night.

Single Manager for Air

Finally, a major problem that continually hindered efficient targeting in air operations over Southeast Asia again surfaced during Linebacker II. In fact, the need for a single command agency for air resources was even more apparent during Linebacker II because for the first time in US air operations against the North Vietnam heartland, a full range of weapon systems was available. The aircraft and ordnance were capable of all-weather operations, area bombing, or pin-point bombing. This capability, however, was degraded by the lack of a single commander for air. In several instances, the less than optimal mix of aircraft and ordnance used resulted in limited damage. For example, the use of B-52s or F-111s against power plants and radcom facilities (small pin-point targets) is much less productive than strikes by terminally guided ordnance. In the case of the Hanoi transmitter, Me Tri prestrike weaponeering indicated an expected 32 percent probability of damage (PD) for 26 B-52s on the main transmitter building; yet eight F-4s using LGBs would have provided an expected 99.6 percent PD.

Additionally, the separation of the strike effort by geographical areas (with Air Force fighter-attack strikes confined to one area of North Vietnam and US Navy strikes to the other) prevented optimal integration of forces and ordnance in each of the areas. The complexity of command and control for employment of B-52s was also a major problem. Scheduling and support of B-52 strikes required constant coordination between major command elements including the Strategic Air Command, COMUSMACV, Headquarters 7th Air Force in Vietnam, and the Navy's Task Force 77 in the Gulf of Tonkin. A single command authority controlling all air assets could have better insured proper allocation of air resources to various areas and made maximum use of aircraft and ordnance mixes.

Campaign Impact

Despite poor weather and an already diversified North Vietnamese logistic system, Linebacker II successfully achieved the stated objective of maximum sustained pressure on the Hanoi and Haiphong complex.

The large and concentrated strike effort on the relatively small area of the Hanoi environs in the limited time frame was completely unprecedented in Southeast Asia air operations. The impact of the campaign was obvious in the severe damage to the North Vietnamese logistic and war-supporting capability. Coupled with the results of Linebacker I, the overall air campaign against North Vietnam resulted in the complete disruption of rail traffic within 10 nautical miles of Hanoi and a serious degradation of rail movement on the northeast rail line and the Thai Nguyen rail loop. The major rail-associated warehouse complexes were all severely damaged, adding to the disruption of logistic movement while strikes on other key storage facilities seriously impaired North Vietnam's efforts to restock necessary supplies.

The psychological effect of Linebacker II operations is extremely difficult to measure. There were indications (government evacuation of school children, nonessential civilian workers, and government offices in early December) that the North Vietnamese anticipated renewed bombing of the heartland. The intensity of US air operations, however, was surely greater than they expected, and some reports indicated that for the first time in the war, people were anxious to leave the cities. Undoubtedly, the population's morale declined as a result of the sheer intensity of the strikes. Reports indicated that US air strikes in the Gia Lam area had a marked psychological effect on the employees at the airport, as many were seen wandering around completely disoriented. Additionally, after the strikes, foreigners were permitted to walk anywhere in the normally restricted airport area. Although reports of this nature were limited, similar instances undoubtedly occurred throughout the target areas in and around Hanoi and Haiphong. Despite such reports, there was no evidence indicating that the North Vietnamese leadership could not have maintained control of the situation. However, it should be noted that the North Vietnamese did return to the peace conference table following Linebacker II.

Notes

1. These results were originally reported in a Headquarters Pacific Air Forces document of the same title, dated April 1973.

2. Headquarters Pacific Air Forces, "Linebacker II Air Operations Summary," March 1973.

3. The study this section is based upon focused only on US Air Force strike results since poststrike photography for US Navy and Marine strikes was not then available. The Navy and Marines flew some 400 strike sorties, 19 percent of the total, during the 12-day period concentrating in the Haiphong area.

4. Headquarters Pacific Air Forces, "Linebacker II Target Damage File," no date. This unpublished file contains target descriptions, damage assessments, and photography for each target struck by the US Air Force during Linebacker II.

5. Ibid.

6. For an excellent discussion of B-52 crew views of Linebacker II strike operations, see George B. Allison and James R. McCarthy, *Linebacker II: A View from the Rock* (Washington, D.C.: Government Printing Office, 1979).

7. "Linebacker II Air Operations Summary," 31.

THIS PAGE INTENTIONALLY LEFT BLANK

Chapter 6

On War, Time, and the
Principle of Substitution

Out of the conflict in Southeast Asia emerged once again evidence
of the subtle but powerful role that substitution plays in the art of
warfare. Traditionally, nations under attack—given sufficient time—
have effected both product and factor substitution to a degree that in
large measure attenuated the economic impact of military strikes against
their industrial and logistic sectors. Seldom has a wartime economy
been so fully mobilized and fine-tuned that the loss of a single part or
function could not in some way be compensated for through the process
of substitution. Franklin's "horseshoe nail" dictum, so applicable in
time-sensitive, tactical situations, loses much of its relevance over the
long term. This fact was particularly true of the protracted war in
Southeast Asia.

Substitution in warfare, of course, is not a recent phenomenon.
History abounds with examples of belligerent nations taking advantage
of this age-old principle. For example, until this century, the process of
converting plowshares into swords was quite characteristic of military
preparations for warfare; advancements in peacetime technology were
later incorporated into the development of military hardware. John Nef,
in his evaluation of warfare and industrialism, concluded that "many
weapons, from the crossbow to the bayonet, were apparently invented,
not for war but for the chase . . . it was not until the nineteenth century
that war replaced sport as the leading stimulus to technical
improvements in firearms"[1] and that "saltpeter and gunpowder appear
in Western history as by-products of remarkable general progress in
knowledge for peaceful purposes."[2] Gunpowder was initially used
during the twelfth century to blast through stone encountered at lead

---

Previously published in *Air University Review* 30, no. 6 (September-October 1979).

and silver mines. It was not until two centuries later that we find references of its use for military purposes in the tubes of cannon. The technology for producing the cannon themselves was derived from the peaceful endeavor of casting church bells, first noted in the eleventh century.[3]

As the demands of warfare increased through the seventeenth century and plowshares were increasingly converted into swords, many European nations found themselves short of the vital metals required for military hardware. It therefore became necessary to reduce the more decorative and extravagant uses of this limited resource. The utility of armor, for instance, had by that time been largely undermined by the evolution in firearms—the warrior of the day could no longer be protected at a weight that did not restrict his mobility. Consequently, the last vestiges of armor were eliminated from the equipment of soldiers, and even the manufacture of breastplates was abandoned. The metal thus saved was used to produce the required firearms. Along this same line, Gustavus Adolphus is said to have sponsored several new models of light artillery—one a so-called leather gun that consisted of a thin copper or bronze tube strengthened with iron rings and covered with a leather skin.[4] Although the primary purpose of his innovations may have been to provide the king's infantry units with maneuverable firepower, they also enabled him to conserve scarce metals. Substitutions such as these let warfare continue, but on an admittedly more limited scale than would have prevailed if the nations of that age had possessed more advanced scientific and administrative skills— factors that in large measure determine the extent to which substitution can be carried.[5]

Our Experience with Germany

The art of substitution in warfare, further developed over the centuries, was applied with remarkable success by the more advanced nations during World War II. In one sense, this result was contingent on the advent of air power and its application deep behind enemy lines against target systems that were only indirectly and in the long term related to battlefield success. Given sufficient time, plus some slack in its economy, a nation can normally improvise and adjust for strategic shortages that might be created. Germany and Great Britain, for instance, were particularly adept at compensating for shortages during most of the war.

Let us look at the German experience a bit more closely. Burton Klein, in his classic study of Germany's wartime economy, concluded that for the first five years of World War II the German economy contained considerable slack.[6] It was not until after the Battle of Stalingrad and the initiation of large-scale raids on its cities at the beginning of 1943 that Germany was shocked into the reality of total war and began to mobilize fully its national resources. From that time until mid-1944, the peak of its war effort, munitions production increased by nearly 50 percent. During the same period, the gradually expanding British and US air effort exacted only a 5 to 10 percent reduction in military output. Beginning in the summer of 1944, however, the tremendous weight of increased Allied air attacks, territorial losses, and manpower problems made further increases of military output impossible; subsequently, these factors brought about Germany's economic collapse. Still, by December 1944 total industrial production was within 15 percent of peak output, and munitions production had fallen by only 18 percent.

After the end of the year, military production rapidly collapsed, and by March, the last month's production data were collected, munitions production was 45 percent below the December level. But paradoxically, states Klein, "even in March 1945, Germany's total military output was at a substantially higher rate than when she began her attack on Russia—an attack which was to have brought complete victory by the summer of 1941."[7]

Although Klein gives Hitler's Nazi regime relatively low marks in its economic preparation for war, he still admired the resilience of the German economy. "What the Germans really excelled in was in improvising. The measures taken to get around the shortage of ferroalloys were truly ingenious. The kinds of measures taken to restore production after bombing attacks and the speed with which production was restored were remarkable."[8]

From an incisive evaluation of target selection during the Combined
Bomber Offensive by Mancur Olson, Jr., we gain further insight into
the capability of the German economy to withstand for so long the Allied
strategic air campaign.[9] Two distinct hypotheses were promoted during
the bomber offensive. The British advocated area bombing of cities on
the premise that the German economy was so fully and efficiently
mobilized that any transfer of resources for either civilian or industrial
restoration would subtract from the war effort. There is now, however,
an impressive array of evidence that area bombing did not decisively
affect either industrial production or the German will to resist.

John Kenneth Galbraith, who along with his other accomplishments
was a director of the US Strategic Bombing Survey, cites as an example
the bombing of Hamburg.[10] For three nights the Royal Air Force
Bomber Command subjected the city of Hamburg to devastating
attacks. A third of the city was destroyed, and at least 60,000 persons
were killed. The industrial plants that were around the edge of the city,
however, were not greatly damaged, and after several weeks of
adjustment, production was back to normal. In fact, many persons
previously engaged in nonessential occupations in the destroyed portion
of the city turned to the war industries for employment, thus alleviating
a former labor shortage. Galbraith concludes that "in reducing, as
nothing else could, the consumption of nonessentials and the
employment of men in their supply, there is a distinct possibility that
the attacks on Hamburg increased Germany's output of war material
and thus her military effectiveness."[11]

The American command favored selective or precision bombing, but
these attacks met with mixed results. Planners first searched for the
small single "horseshoe nail" target system that, if destroyed, would
cause a virtual stoppage of all military production. The selection of the
ball bearing industry appeared a logical choice. Attacks on these plants
alone were to reduce German armaments production by 30 percent, and
since production was concentrated in relatively few cities, the industry
could be easily destroyed. In the subsequent raids, about one-half of the
industry's floorspace was destroyed and another half severely damaged,
yet Germany's capacity to wage war was not impaired. A limited
amount of dispersal had already taken place, and losses in output were

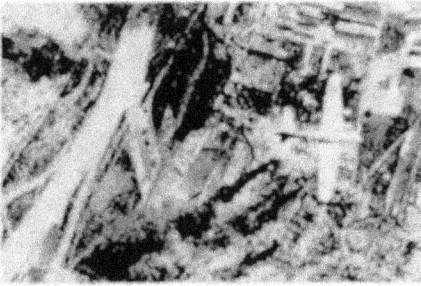

AXIS OIL FACILITIES

During World War II, primary target systems in Germany and Axis Europe of Allied bombing were the synthetic oil plants and dumps. An oil blending plant suffered heavy damage. . . . Also frequently attacked in the bombings were such plants as the Xenia and Romana oil refineries at Ploesti, center of the important Romanian oil fields.

restored between raids much more quickly than US experts believed possible. Moreover, the Germans were able to manage with fewer ball bearings than anticipated through redesign of equipment and the reduction of excessive and often luxurious uses of bearings.[12]

Olson feels that the economist's fundamental theory of substitution explains the shortcomings of both strategies. In the case of area bombing, the British could not expect to destroy more than a small proportion of a large number of industries. But when only "a small proportion of the productive capacity of an industry is destroyed, this capacity can be spared or replaced particularly easily."[13] For selective bombing, the search for the small but indispensable industry proved illusionary. "The enemy could always afford to replace most of any industry if that industry was small enough. And it matters not how 'essential' an industry might be if the enemy can easily replace that industry once it has been destroyed."[14]

Contrast the results against the ball bearing industry, for example, with the success experienced in strikes against the German synthetic oil industry. These raids, coming during the final year of the war, put a tremendous strain on the German economic system. Throughout the war, oil had been exceedingly expensive and in short supply. Having been cut off from their primary sources, the Germans had developed a synthetic process for making oil out of coal. The synthetic oil industry was large, extremely costly, and critically important to the war effort. Destruction of this industry, which was already a substitute for a missing source of supply, foreclosed the opportunity to improvise further. Time had run out, and the limits of substitution had been reached.[15]

Our Experience with North Vietnam

With the preceding historical survey as background, let us now turn to the more recent conflict in Southeast Asia and investigate the role that substitution played in the ability of North Vietnam to withstand US strategic air attacks. In contrast to Germany, North Vietnam at the start of the air war was essentially an agricultural country with only a rudimentary transportation system and little modern industry of any kind. More than 90 percent of the population lived in primitive villages and earned their living from the soil. Less than 2 percent were engaged in industry, and only the capital city of Hanoi and the port city of Haiphong had populations of more than 100,000.

The gradual escalation of the bombing campaign in the north provided the North Vietnamese ample time and opportunity to make appropriate adjustments and institute countermeasures to the destruction rendered from the air. Both the military logistic system and the civilian economy converted to highly dispersed and decentralized methods of storing and handling supplies. The Vietnamese constructed hundreds of miles of highway bypasses and alternate routes and

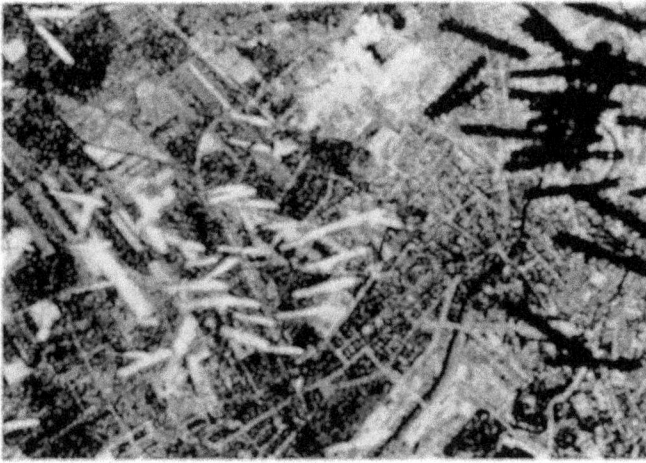

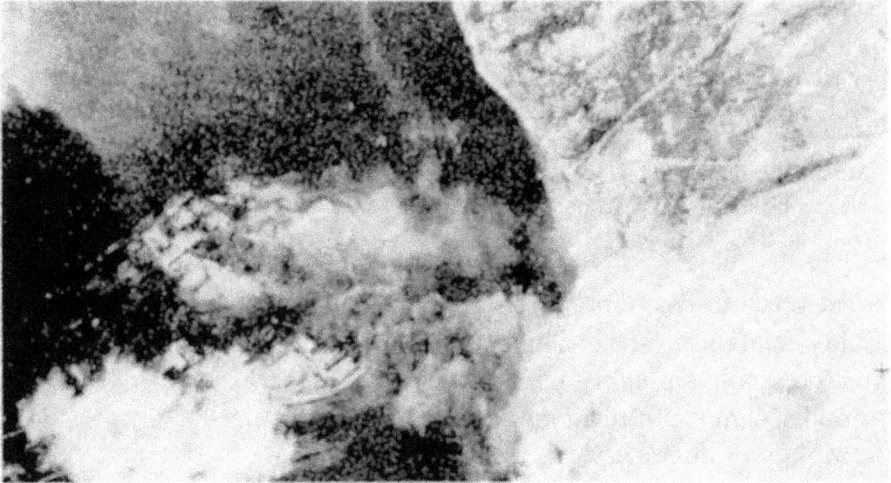

High on the priority list of targets for Eighth Air Force daylight bombing during World War II were Germany's largest rubber factories at Hanover. . . . The great Vahrenwalder-Strasse tire factory was bombed by both the RAF and the Eighth's heavy bombers, by the latter on 26 July 1943; 21 direct hits resulted in smoke columns as high as 22,000 feet in the air.

improved the carrying capacity of the railroad network by converting it to dual gauge. Inland waterways were improved, and bridges were replaced by fords and alternate structures less vulnerable to air attacks. Construction material, equipment, and workers were positioned at advantageous locations along key routes to effect quick repairs.

Harrison Salisbury, the *New York Times* correspondent who visited Hanoi in December 1966, observed at firsthand many of the repair activities instituted by the North Vietnamese.[16] The highways were rapidly repaired by simply filling in the bomb craters with native clay soil. The North Vietnamese repaired railroads with steel rails, ties, and crushed gravel that had been positioned along the full length of the roadbeds. More challenging were the bridges, but on this subject Salisbury cites some impressive examples of North Vietnamese ingenuity:

> If the bridge was completely knocked out, a pontoon was put into service. The pontoons could not have been simpler in concept or easier to put into place. They were made by lashing together the required number of shallow flat-bottomed wooden canal boats, of which there were countless numbers available along the canals and streams. These sturdy boats, three feet wide and perhaps sixteen feet long, made an excellent bridge. A surface of cut bamboo poles was laid across them, without even being lashed or nailed in many cases. Or, if available, a surface of bamboo planks. The trucks lumbered over the pontoons with a roar as their wheels hit the loose poles, but the pontoons seemed sturdy enough to bear the heavy traffic.[17]

The boats and bamboo were stored in the vicinity of every bridge and could be put into place in a matter of hours. Moreover, these temporary structures could quickly be removed and hidden in the morning to minimize damage from air raids and reinstalled in the evening to handle the nightly truck traffic.

The problem of keeping the railroads open was more difficult since the trains could not run across pontoons, but here again native ingenuity came into play:

> If the rail line was blocked by destruction of a bridge or trackage, bicycle brigades were called up. Five hundred men and women and their bicycles would be sent to the scene of the break. They would unload the stalled freight train, putting the cargo on the bikes. Each bicycle would handle a six-hundred pound load, balanced

across the frame with a bar. The bicycles would be wheeled, not ridden, over a pontoon bridge, and on the other side of the break a second train would be drawn up. The cargo would be reloaded and moved on south.[18]

In addition to the above, Salisbury observed the grand scale to which fuels, supplies, and equipment were dispersed to make them less vulnerable to air attack. "Indeed, in all the time I rode about the countryside I think I was never more than two or three minutes out of sight of some kind of supplies and equipment which had come to rest in the most unlikely setting."[19] Fifty-five-gallon drums in which petroleum was stored, repair equipment, and crates containing weapons, munitions, and other hardware were randomly dispersed throughout the fields, rice paddies, and villages. Naturally this dispersal was costly to Hanoi in terms of both manpower and materiel, but it was a price the government willingly paid to continue the war effort.

Although only 15 percent of North Vietnam's gross national product was provided by industry, portions of the industrial sector were also dispersed, and many city residents were evacuated to the countryside. In the main, however, North Vietnam depended on imports from the Communist bloc for industrial products. Whereas Germany substituted alternate processes and materials to satisfy its industrial needs, North Vietnam substituted foreign aid to satisfy its. The North Vietnamese operated much as the Dutch had done in the sixteenth century when they defended themselves successfully for more than 80 years against the strongest arms in Europe. Having few natural materials themselves, the Dutch employed their greatest resources, "the sea with its inlets, the good harbors and rivers, and the inland waterways which they built . . . to get from Sweden, northern Germany, England, and Scotland the materials which they needed to defend themselves."[20] Both nations substituted foreign production for their own. In this sense, North Vietnam functioned more as a logistic funnel than as a production base for operations in the south.

Some production, of course, did take place, but this production was mostly of simple consumer essentials improvised by small-scale industry and handicrafts. A Hanoi news report, for instance, claimed that in one province "the population has collected 27 tons of bomb and rocket fragments to be worked on by the local smithies, who turned them into more than 16,000 plowshares."[21] If true, this practice is another example of the substitution effected by the North Vietnamese for limited natural resources.

The North Vietnamese also seem to have handled their manpower problems quite adequately. With the passage of time, of course, tasks that are novel at first and must be met with untested people become routine. As a result of this factor alone, by 1966 Hanoi probably had a substantial and valuable investment in learning, practice, and experience.[22] Moreover, the quality of the manpower base was further improved through formal training programs provided both in-country and abroad.[23] Whatever technical skills that still remained in short supply were imported from other Communist nations.[24]

An adequate supply of labor was assured through several programs. Curtailment and suspension of nonessential civilian activities released some workers for the war effort, but it appears that the most common practice was to exact double duty from the laborers. In-country combat tasks were performed on top of, rather than instead of, other employment. Production workers in plants substituted as air defense gunners during air raids. Beside each production position was a rifle, and when the siren sounded, the workers would grab their rifles and take up posts at windows or on the roof to fire at US planes. Agricultural workers substituted as repair crews when called on by local authorities to assist in repairing bombed-out roads and railroads. Salisbury even cites what would appear to be an extreme example of North Vietnamese Air Force pilots' arising at 4 a.m., working in the rice paddies for three or four hours, and then flying their planes against the Americans.[25]

The last example may not be so far-fetched given the specialized and constrained pattern of the US air campaign at that time. In fact, the air strikes, normally conducted near midday, fashioned the whole lifestyle around Hanoi. Commercial activity thrived from 5 to 8 a.m., after which shops closed and did not open again until late afternoon. By 6 p.m. activity was again at a high level, and the streets, beer parlors, and bars were jammed.[26]

Salisbury's observations lead one to believe that there was still considerable slack in the North Vietnamese labor force in 1966. Obviously, commercial and recreational pursuits had not been greatly curtailed. He also noted that there had been an increase of from 80,000 to 100,000 high school students and from 35,000 to 46,000 college students in the last year.[27] Although these students participated in part-time agricultural and military functions, they were still an untapped labor source for an all-out effort. It is, of course, difficult to determine how many persons were engaged either full or part-time in war-related activities in North Vietnam, but one Rand analyst guessed that the number might run from 1 to 1.5 million men and women, including the military. If this estimate is correct, only about 10 to 15 percent of the able-bodied adult population was so occupied.[28]

Most industrial and logistic processes require some combination of labor and capital as inputs. Within limits, one can be substituted for the other. As an example, human portering, in many situations, is a viable alternative to rail or truck transport. If capital has been destroyed or is in short supply, a nation with a sufficient manpower base will normally turn to more labor-intensive methods to maintain a given level of output. The bicycle brigades employed to transport supplies past destroyed railroad bridges and the very labor-intensive dispersal techniques cited by Salisbury are two good illustrations. With an apparently abundant labor force, the North Vietnamese were able to make many such substitutions in their continuing support of the conflict in the South.

Some Comparisons

There exists a general consensus that the bombing of the North from 1965 until November 1968 failed to alter significantly North Vietnam's ability or will to continue the war.[29] What then went wrong? Why was the world's greatest power unable to bomb an essentially second-rate nation into submission? Most experts believe that the failure was due primarily to three factors. First, North Vietnam supported operations in the South mainly by functioning as a logistic funnel: a majority of the equipment and supplies came from other Communist nations. Second, as indicated above, North Vietnam possessed a manpower base of sufficient size to effect any labor-intensive substitutions required for continuation of the war. Finally, the volume of supplies needed in the

Vietnam, 1967

In Vietnam, USAF B-52s dropped bombs from extremely high altitudes on unsuspecting ground troop sanctuaries, keeping enemy forces on the move. . . . Frequent targets of concentrated attack were petroleum, oil, and lubricant (POL) storage facilities and transportation systems. At the Thai Nguyen barge construction area, bridge sections and POL tanks were assembled.

South was so low that only a small portion of the capacity of North Vietnam's redundant and flexible transportation system was required to maintain the flow.

There also can be no denying that the gradual escalation of the bombing campaign gave the North Vietnamese time to improvise, adjust, and develop the necessary countermeasures that in large measure attenuated the bombing impact. Note, for example, the following excerpt from a 1967 North Vietnamese military analysis:

> The might of the U.S. Air Force lies in the fact that it has many planes, modern technical means, bombs and bullets, and available airfields in Thailand and South Vietnam, and at sea. It can attack us from many directions on many targets, under different weather conditions, by day and by night. However, given their political isolation and the present balance of international forces, the U.S. Air Force is compelled to escalate step by step, and cannot attack the North massively and swiftly in strategic, large-scale, surprise bombings. Our North Vietnam can gain the time and circumstances necessary to gradually transform the country to a war footing, to further develop its forces, and to gain experience in order to deal the U.S. Air Force heavier blows.[30]

Time, then, becomes the essential factor that dilutes the effect of strategic warfare. Only when an economic system is critically strained and time is running out can the type of bombing campaigns described in this chapter succeed in achieving their desired results. This fact can be illustrated with the three target systems that received the most concentrated attacks in Southeast Asia: hydroelectric power complexes; petroleum, oil, and lubricants (POL) storage facilities; and lines of communication (the transportation system).

In the almost four-year bombing campaign (1965-68), over 80 percent of the central electric generating capacity of North Vietnam was either destroyed or rendered inoperable; yet there was sufficient redundancy in the system to permit the most essential operations to be continued. Possessing only a limited industrial base, North Vietnam, of course, did not require a huge amount of electric power. Moreover, all critical elements of its military and governmental agencies had alternative means of generating electricity. Even during the large B-52 raids in December 1972, when all Hanoi's major power sources were rendered inoperable and the capacity available from the national power grid was reduced by some 75 percent, electricity continued to be supplied to priority users, such as selected government buildings, important industrial installations, and foreign embassies.[31] In summary, then, the essential requirements for electric power did not put an overbearing strain on the remaining capacity, and the redundancy in the system permitted the North Vietnamese to substitute for destroyed and damaged power elements.

The results against POL storage facilities were similar although the underlying substitution mechanism was quite different. North Vietnam had no capability to generate additional POL internally; however, it could obtain the required stocks elsewhere. This form of substitution is illustrated in the assessment of the concentrated POL strikes conducted in 1966. Although the intelligence community estimated that 70 percent of North Vietnamese storage capacity had been destroyed, it concluded, "There is no evidence yet of any shortage of POL in North Vietnam and stocks on hand, with recent imports, have been adequate to sustain necessary operations."[32] The North Vietnamese were able to supplement their reduced reserves immediately with imports of more POL products. Outside aid was substituted for a missing source of supply, and operations were continued.

Contrast these results with those achieved against the German synthetic oil industry by Allied air strikes during World War II. Coming as they did when POL was critically needed by the Germans in their effort to halt advancing Allied ground forces, these strikes severely crippled the German war machine. The oil industry was large and costly, and there was insufficient time to develop an alternate source of supply. Consequently, the German war effort rapidly collapsed.

The third target system, lines of communication, received by far the greatest weight of effort. Strikes against lines of communication were conducted not only around Hanoi and Haiphong, the general area on which the previous discussion has concentrated, but also in the lower panhandle of North Vietnam above the demilitarized zone and along the Ho Chi Minh Trail of southern Laos, where strikes were concentrated after the November 1968 bombing halt in North Vietnam. Although the strikes against the industrial base and energy sources already described might more appropriately be termed strategic bombardment, the strikes against lines of communication fell into the interdiction category. These strikes took two forms: attacks of delay against the railroad and road network itself and attacks of destruction against vehicles and supplies on the network. The purpose of these strikes was to reduce the flow of men and materiel to a level below that at which offensive operations in the South could be maintained.

Since the initiation of air interdiction missions during World War II, these strikes have been the most controversial of all air power missions. Unless they are executed concurrent with major ground operations in which the enemy is forced into a high expenditure rate, it is difficult to prove that they significantly influence the outcome of a battle. Notable successes were registered during World War II and the first year of the Korean conflict, but with the advent of protracted war in which there is no clear outcome, it has been virtually impossible to establish a positive payoff for these strikes. Guerrilla warfare requires only a minimum of supplies, and since the option to fight or withdraw remains open, the volume and timing of replacements are not vital to success.

Although the true impact of interdiction in Southeast Asia may never be known with certainty, I feel that it was within the range of North Vietnamese tolerance.[33] Admittedly, political restraints against a full-scale interdiction effort, including naval blockade, mitigated the effect of the US effort. Yet, Communist needs in South Vietnam were not great—not more than 50 tons a day were required from the Ho Chi Minh Trail—and they could easily make whatever adjustments were necessary within their logistic system to keep this amount flowing and to accumulate a surplus for future operations.

To be sure, the North Vietnamese were fighting a protracted war, and a protracted war implies time. With time, substitution becomes a viable option. Temporary structures replace destroyed bridges, bypasses circumnavigate interdicted route segments, and men and materiel are diverted from less essential to more critical functions. The operations and repair activities Harrison Salisbury observed were characteristic of North Vietnam's efforts along these lines. The North Vietnamese transportation capacity was more than adequate for the type of war they were fighting, and time was not a critical factor. This set of circumstances was quite different from the one in which the Germans found themselves during the final year of World War II. According to Olson:

> The German railroad industry was strained to the maximum near the end of the war by the demands at the front and the extra transport required because of the dispersal of factories subject to the bombing attack. Thus, when this industry was bombed repeatedly and mercilessly, the Germans had nothing to turn to but canal transport, truck transport, and air transport. But by this time the Nazi beast had been cornered: the canals were breached at the same time, while trucks could not run for lack of oil and the allies had control of the air.[34]

As with the German oil industry, time had run out, and the opportunity of substitution had been foreclosed.

Of the primary target systems struck in Germany during World War II, the most notable successes were scored against the synthetic oil and transportation industries. Both of these industries were large and costly, making them difficult to replace. Perhaps an even more important factor is that the weight of effort against these industries came in the final year of the war when the German economic system was severely strained. Following the successful Allied invasion of Normandy, German forces were heavily committed on two fronts, and the resulting demands placed on the German war machine were tremendous. There was insufficient time remaining to create substitutes for these industries even if the capability existed. The situation was quite similar to that in which Japan found itself at the end of World War II. Faced with a highly compressed, intensive bombing campaign against its industrial base and an impending Allied invasion which it no longer had the means to repel, Japan soon capitulated.

Primary elements in the conduct of warfare, then, must be both the time and ability to make successful substitutions. Given these two factors, a nation can go a long way toward mitigating the impact of the most devastating bombing attacks. And so it was with the North Vietnamese. Only in the latter part of 1972, after strikes against the North were resumed and the flow of imports was restricted, was there any evidence of a reduction in the North Vietnamese ability or will to continue the fight. But by that time the North Vietnamese Army had suffered severe losses in an imprudent invasion of the South.

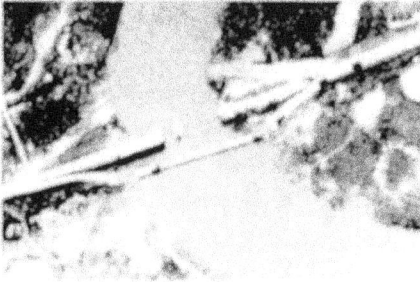

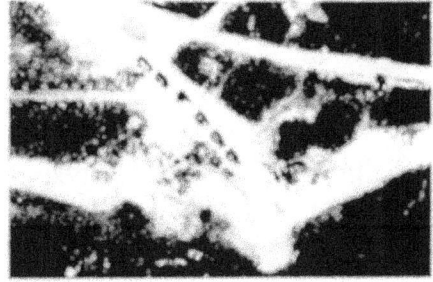

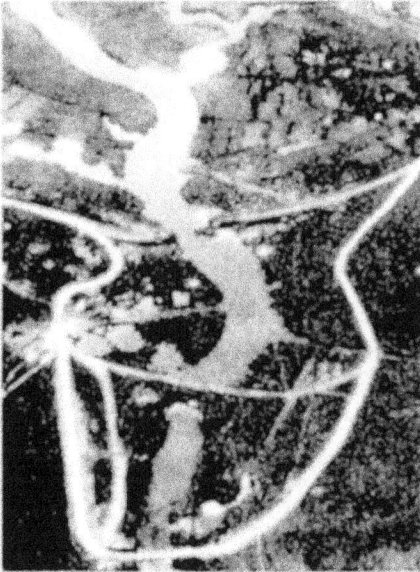

THE SUBSTITUTION PRINCIPLE

The North Vietnamese made any adjustments necessary to continue the fight. Air attacks along Route 1A pitted the road, but it was soon repaired and cargo trucks waited at the ferry crossing. . . . Trucks cross over a pontoon bridge, bypassing the bombed out Dong Lac highway bridge. . . . Although repeated bombings had destroyed the bridges and roads along this important North Vietnamese supply route, bypass routes were quickly constructed, including new bridges.

As Olson makes quite clear in his evaluation of target selection during the Combined Bombing Offensive, "it was not that air power could not destroy what it set out to destroy: the problem was rather that what it destroyed was not after all indispensable. The fault was not one of airmanship, it was one of economics."[35] Given time, a resource they possessed in abundance, the North Vietnamese were able to make those substitutions necessary to their continued participation in the conflict. Surely, the cost of operations increased as one type of labor, good, or process was continually substituted for another, thus giving rise to the law of diminishing returns. Yet, for the most part, labor was plentiful, and materiel needs could be satisfied through increased imports.

Whatever costs were incurred could be paid by cutting down on nonessential production and consumption.

History is replete with examples such as those described. Most industrial and logistic systems were far more resilient than originally assumed. Prewar assessments on substitutability have been predicated almost entirely on the availability of materials and processes existing in peacetime economies. Only when wartime necessity forces their discovery do many substitution possibilities become known.[36] An equally important consideration, however, is that most assessments have also failed to make adequate allowance for the mitigating effect of time. Consequently, strategic plans based on these assessments have not succeeded, at least to the degree originally conceived.

What is called for is a return to the concept of blitzkrieg. The blitzkrieg model would appear to be the logical foundation on which to base US conventional war strategy. The greatest successes of both air and ground forces in modern times have come in short, intense combined arms campaigns: the German blitzkriegs of World War II, the Normandy invasion, the Six-Day War in the Mideast, and most recently, Desert Storm, to name a few. These successes suggest that military doctrine should be structured so that air power is used in conjunction with other forces in fast and dramatic moves which give no opportunity for the principle of substitution to come into play. It was with such a strategy that Hitler quickly conquered almost the whole of Europe. And it was when he deviated from this strategy that he began to fail.

Notes

1. John U. Nef, *War and Human Progress* (Cambridge, Mass.: Harvard University Press, 1950), 129.

2. Ibid., 27.

3. Ibid., 26–28.

4. Ibid., 239.

5. Mancur Olson, Jr., "American Materials Policy and the 'Physiocratic Fallacy,'" *Orbis*, Winter 1963, 682–83; hereafter cited as "American Materials Policy."

6. Burton H. Klein, *Germany's Economic Preparations for War* (Cambridge, Mass.: Harvard University Press, 1959). See pages 225–38 for a fuller treatment of material cited herein.

7. Ibid., 229.

8. Ibid., 236.

9. Mancur Olson, Jr., "The Economics of Target Selection for the Combined Bomber Offensive," *The Royal United Service Institution Journal*, November 1962; hereafter cited as "The Economics of Target Selection." I am indebted to Olson for much of the discussion that follows.

10. John K. Galbraith, *The Affluent Society* (New York: The New World Library, 1958), 131–33.

11. Ibid., 132.

12. As with ball bearings, the Germans were able to alleviate many shortages by improvising and substituting plentiful for scarce resources. Copper was saved by substituting iron radiators for copper radiators in motor vehicles and by cutting the amount of copper used in U-boats and locomotives by 50 and 90 percent, respectively. Alloys using scarce metals, such as nickel and molybdenum, were replaced with alloys using plentiful metals, such as vanadium, in critical products like gun tubes. For other substitutions, see Olson, "American Materials Policy," and Edward S. Mason, "American Security and Access to Raw Materials," *World Politics*, January 1949.

13. Olson, "The Economics of Target Selection," 313.

14. Ibid., 132.

15. Albert Speer believes that the campaign against the ball bearing industry would also have been successful if it were not for the long pauses between the major raids of August 1943, October 1943, and February-March 1944 in which some production was restored. This restoration is, however, but another example of time's role in strategic successes and failures. Albert Speer, *Inside the Third Reich* (New York: Macmillan, 1970), 339–41.

16. Harrison E. Salisbury, *Behind the Lines—Hanoi* (New York: Harper and Row, 1967), 86–91.

17. Ibid., 88.

18. Ibid., 89. Although railroad repair was more difficult than road repair, the North Vietnamese maintained the railroads in case gasoline and oil imports were cut off. Locomotives were fueled with local coal and wood.

19. Ibid., 91.

20. Nef, 117.

21. Quoted in Oleg Hoeffding, *Bombing North Vietnam: An Appraisal of Economic and Political Effects,* Rand Report RM-5213 (Santa Monica, Calif.: The Rand Corporation, December 1966), footnote, p. 29.

22. Ibid., 15.

23. North Vietnamese sources claimed that nearly 80,000 technical workers and cadres were graduated in North Vietnam in 1965 and that 5,000 North Vietnamese were being trained in Communist countries. Ibid., footnotes on pages 8 and 16.

24. An estimated 40,000 Chinese engineers and construction workers, for example, were employed on the railroads. Ibid., footnote, p. 8.

25. Salisbury, 145.

26. Ibid., 113–14.

27. Ibid., 129–30.

28. Hoeffding, 7.

29. *The Pentagon Papers: The Senator Gravel Edition*, vol. 4 (Boston: Beacon Press, 1971).

30. Quoted in Patrick J. McGarvey, *Visions of Victory: Selected Vietnamese Military Writings, 1964–1968* (Stanford, Calif.: Hoover Institution Press, 1959), 156.

31. See chapter 5.

32. *Pentagon Papers*, vol. 4, 111.

33. See chapter 2.

34. Olson, "The Economics of Target Selection," 313.

35. Ibid., 310.

36. Carl Kaysen, *Notes on the Strategic Air Intelligence in World War II (ETO)*, Rand Report R-165 (Santa Monica, Calif.: The Rand Corporation, October 1949), 14–15.

Index

Laser-guided bombing: 78, 81, 84, 97–101, 105, 109
Linebacker, Operation (10 May 1972–23 October 1972): 81, 111, 114; Easter Offensive (1972) and: 3, 4, 21
Linebacker II, Operation (18–29 December 1972): 5–6, 75, 107, 113–14
Lines of communication: 1, 16, 21, 37–38, 52, 131
Logistics: 11, 15, 22, 24–26, 28, 34–35
LORAN (long-range aid to navigation): 78, 84, 87–89, 97, 100, 109–10

MACV (United States Military Assistance Command, Vietnam): 24; commander: 65, 72, 113
MK-36: 83, 85
MK-82: 99
MK-84: 85, 87, 99
Monsoons. *See* Weather

Navy, carriers: 61; naval air support: 62; naval blockade: 131
North Vietnam: 2, 68, 113; Air Force: 73; Army: 63

Operations. *See* specific operations
Overlord, Operation: 11

Rolling Thunder, Operation: 1–2

Single manager for air, lack of: 113

Sortie counts: 52
South Vietnam: 2; Air Force: 62–63, 72
Strangle, Operation: 8–10, 27
Strategic Air Command (SAC): 113; B-52 operations in Southeast Asia: 61
Strike sorties: 2, 5, 34–35, 62, 71, 76, 84, 86, 90
Substitution in warfare: 117–34; Germany: 118–20; manpower: 126–27; North Vietnam: 122, 130

Targets: 35, 89, 129; airfields: 76, 88–89, 103, 108; bridges: 93–95; damage, overall: 96–99, 103–10; destruction: 33; industrial: 13, 28, 122, 130; petroleum, oil, and lubricants (POL): 129–30; power facilities: 76, 87–88, 96, 104, 129; radio communications facilities: 75, 84–85, 96, 104, 129; railroad yards: 77, 81, 96, 103, 110; SAM sites: 76, 90–91, 104, 108, 112; selection: 91; storage areas: 37, 45, 81–83, 96, 103–4, 110; transshipment points: 81–82

Transportation, enemy: 9, 16, 18, 35; railroad and highway network: 11, 33, 37, 45, 75–77, 81, 83, 93-94, 114, 124, 131

Weather: 15, 21–22, 39, 42, 68, 78, 96, 100–102, 106, 109, 111
World War II: 6, 8, 16, 131, 134